Baby's First Year Journal

Baby's First Year Journal

A Day-to-Day Guide to Your Baby's Development
During the First Twelve Months

A. CHRISTINE HARRIS, PH.D.

ILLUSTRATIONS BY GREG STADLER

CHRONICLE BOOKS
SAN FRANCISCO

This Chronicle Books LLC edition published in 2009.
Text copyright © 1999, 2009 by A. Christine Harris.
Illustrations copyright © 1999, 2009 by Greg Stadler.

ISBN: 978-0-8118-6990-4

Manufactured in China.

Design by Gretchen Scoble.
Illustrations by Greg Stadler.

10 9 8 7 6 5 4 3 2 1

Chronicle Books LLC
680 Second Street
San Francisco, CA 94107

www.chroniclebooks.com

To our sweet grandbaby, Yazmine.

Acknowledgments

I am grateful for the effective professionalism of Allison Arieff,
the original editor of this book, who made this project a joy.
Sincere thanks to librarians Sandra A. Vella at the University of California, Davis,
and Barbara Nuss at Cosumnes River College, who helped with the research.
The support and encouragement of my family sustains me.
Thanks to Bob for everything, to Heather for her interest and affection,
to Wendy for Yazmine and Ariceli, and to Olivia Christine
who reminds me of the delights of baby's first year.

Contents

Preface

At no other time in life are physical changes and developmental achievements as dramatic as during infancy. The growth rate during the first twelve months after birth is faster than at any time thereafter. At the same time the infant develops skills that allow him to begin to recognize and respond to the objects, people, and events that surround him. The sequence of developmental events is basically the same for all babies, but the rate may vary. However, the ultimate attainment of a skill is probably more important than whether any individual child is developing relatively "earlier" or "later" than others. In terms of behavior, individual differences among infants can be significant, while differences among females and males are generally minor.

During infancy three major developmental systems undergo progressive maturation. Physical development depends on overall health and involves changes in height, weight, body proportions, balance, and coordination, and the maturation of the internal systems and tissues. Cognitive development involves the acquisition of knowledge and the development of thinking, reasoning, and problem solving. It depends on the operation of the senses, the processes of attention and perception, and the acquisition of language. Social-emotional development involves the quality of the interactions between the baby and others within a cultural frame-work. It is contingent on the processes of attachment and interpersonal play, and the interactive aspects of communication.

Baby's First Year Journal offers a day-by-day guide to the progress of physical, cognitive, and social-emotional development during baby's first twelve months. It provides places for parents to record their thoughts and observations during this important time. Personalized to baby's own birthday, *Baby's First Year Journal* helps parents anticipate baby's next steps within a framework that takes into account a wide range of typical infant development. In addition, the caregiving strategy for baby's first year detailed on the following pages can help parents optimize baby's developmental progress. (Always consult your health-care provider with any questions or concerns.)

Caregiving Strategy for Baby's First Year

The most essential ingredient in infant care is a warm, responsive, and dependable adult caregiver. Warmth is expressed in time spent holding, cuddling, and interacting with baby. Responding quickly to baby's cries helps him develop a sense of trust and security. Feeling secure encourages baby to try new things. A dependable caregiver behaves in consistent ways, so baby will know what to expect. Warm, responsive, dependable caregivers support and encourage development, but don't push. They make their baby a priority.

Encouraging Physical Development

* Provide interesting things for baby to see, hear, smell, taste, and touch.
* Place baby in different positions so her viewing angle changes.
* Give baby time and space to practice moving her muscles and to develop balance and motor coordination.
* Safeguard baby's health with regular visits to a health-care provider.
* Keep baby safe from accidental or intentional harm.

Encouraging Cognitive Development

* Vary baby's experiences. Expose him to different places and things.
* Encourage language acquisition by providing a language-rich environment.
* Give baby time and space to play on his own.
* Understand the progress of development so you will have realistic expectations regarding what baby can do and understand.
* Help baby learn age-appropriate self-care skills.
* Always remember that you are a model for baby to imitate. Watch what you say and do.

Encouraging Social-Emotional Development

* Love your baby unconditionally. Express your love both verbally and behaviorally.
* Provide a stable, predictable, low-stress environment.
* Help baby develop a sense of trust and security.
* Be responsive to baby's physical and emotional needs.
* Comfort baby and help her comfort herself in times of stress or change.
* Get to know your baby's personality/temperament. How does she respond to people and events? What does she tend to like, dislike, fear, or avoid?
* Play with your baby often.
* Help baby to interact comfortably with others.
* Remember that the quality of the infant-parent relationship is affected by the quality of the parents' relationship with each other.

Discipline

The best way to discipline a baby under a year old is a combination of baby-proofing and distraction. Divert baby's attention from a forbidden item or area by moving him physically to a different location and giving him something to play with.

Spoiling

Parents may wonder whether they should tolerate baby's clinging, dependent behavior, especially if there is pressure from others who view this as "spoiling." Be reassured that baby's clinging is healthy, desirable, and necessary for the infant's optimum emotional development. At each stage of development, baby needs different resources from the family. During the first year, a variety of experiences and the availability of the parents for attachment are primary. Soothing a frightened baby or tolerating clinging does not tend to spoil the baby or reward fearfulness—it's comforting and reassuring, especially if baby is shy or slow to adapt. A caregiver can "spoil" a child by always giving in, never saying no, and not setting reasonable limits.

Parents

* Identify a network of resources that can provide advice, support, and relief.
* Understand that parenting is hard work, rich in joy and frustration.
* Remember that parenting is a learned skill, not a genetic trait or instinct.

Personalizing Baby's First Year Journal

All of the information in this journal is keyed to your baby's own birthday and is chronicled weekly.

For babies born at term (within two weeks of their estimated due date): The easiest way to personalize *Baby's First Year Journal* is to begin with the day baby was born as Day 0 and, using a monthly calendar as a guide, date each day in sequence ending with baby's first birthday. (If the year is a leap year, *Baby's First Year Journal* will end the day before baby's first birthday).

For babies born prematurely: Since developmental age is a better predictor of behavior than chronological age, the premature baby's chronological age should probably be adjusted. It may seem unlikely that three or more weeks could make much developmental difference, but they can because of the accelerated growth that takes place during infancy. Thus, the more accurate baby's developmental age, the more likely information in *Baby's First Year Journal* will reflect baby's actual developmental progress.

If your baby was born prematurely, label the journal as you would for a baby born at term, beginning with the baby's birth date as Day 0. Then, to find the baby's developmental age and the corresponding information, count back from today's date the number of days premature your baby was born from your estimated due date.

Calculating baby's chronological and adjusted age:

EXAMPLE	MONTH	DAY	YEAR		YOUR BABY	MONTH	DAY	YEAR
Estimated due date	11	27	2009		Estimated due date			
Date of birth	11	2	2009		Date of birth			
Number of days premature		25			Number of days premature			
Today's date	12	15	2009		Today's date			
Developmental age date	11	21	2009		Developmental age date			

In the example above, while the baby is about 6 weeks (43 days) old chronologically, he may be better represented developmentally as about 3 weeks (19 days) old.

For babies with special needs: Babies with special needs may lag behind their peers in some aspects of development. Parents are reminded to keep baby's special circumstances in mind as they follow the progress of infant development during the first year.

Your Newborn

APPEARANCE

Head: Headfirst vaginal delivery causes temporary head molding. The forehead may be flattened and sloped back toward a rounded crest at the back of the head. The scalp may be somewhat swollen or ridged.

Skin: Baby may have little or no *vernix* on her skin unless she was premature. Vernix is the substance that coated baby's skin prior to birth to protect it and her developing glands and sensory cells. It takes about twenty-four hours after the first bath for any vernix left on baby's skin to be absorbed.

The newborn's skin is generally loose and wrinkled unless he was particularly large at birth. Baby's forehead, neck, shoulders, and/or back may be covered with a fine, downy hair called *lanugo*, especially if she was premature. The lanugo will disappear within a few weeks or months.

Baby's skin may look red, bright pink, and/or blotchy at first. The skin's true color may not appear for a few hours or a few days. Ninety percent of babies born to parents of African, Indian, or Asian descent are born with gray or slate-blue patches on their lower back and buttocks. Called *Mongolian spots*, these patches generally fade within the first year.

The newborn's face—especially around the nose and chin—may have what look like tiny whiteheads on it. Caused by clogged immature oil glands, these *milia* require no treatment. They will disappear in a few weeks as the oil glands mature.

There may be mocha-colored birthmarks called *café au lait spots* and/or deep red or purplish patches of skin called *port-wine stains*. The most common birthmarks are called *stork bites* or *salmon patches*. These are deep pink areas commonly found on the back of the head or neck, the bridge of the nose, or the eyelids, caused by dilation of the capillaries in those areas. Birthmarks of all types are usually harmless and will become lighter and less noticeable with age—95 percent fade completely by age two.

Color: If your newborn's hands and feet look blue, don't worry. Virtually every newborn's extremities look blue at one time or another, either because he's cold and needs to be covered up or because of the sluggishness of his immature circulation. If the problem persists, or if the baby's torso turns blue, contact the health-care provider.

Eyes: Baby's eyelids may be puffy for the first few days after birth. All newborns routinely receive antibiotic ointment or drops in their eyes immediately after birth to guard against infection and protect vision. As a consequence, baby's eyes may have some discharge or swelling.

Ears: Baby's ears may be folded or pushed out of shape by the birth process. The physical changes in the baby's ears are temporary and do not affect hearing.

Umbilical cord: After birth, the umbilical cord is shortened to about an inch and treated with antiseptic. Until the cord drops off one to four weeks after birth, it's important to keep the stump dry (dabbed with alcohol and exposed to the air), unrestricted by clothing or diaper, and free from infection. Baby should be given a sponge bath rather than a tub bath until the cord falls off.

Swelling: During birth, babies normally receive an abundance of female hormones from the placenta, which causes swelling (and sometimes discharge) in the breast tissue and genitals of both male and female babies. It takes the baby's body several months to rid the excess hormones from his system; no damage is done to male or female tissues.

BEHAVIOR

Breathing: Most newborns are fairly noisy breathers. The rings of cartilage in the windpipe of some newborns aren't fully developed. When air is inhaled or exhaled, the rings make a rattling sound. The sound may be louder when the baby is on her back or side.

Head control: The full-term baby is born with some ability to hold his head erect, but his neck muscles are weak and the head is large and heavy compared to the rest of the body. If the full-term newborn is held up so her body is vertical, she can momentarily hold the head in the midline of the body. When placed on her stomach, she can lift and drag her head from side to side.

Movement: The newborn may accidentally roll over because of his rounded back.

Body posture: At birth, when baby is pulled halfway to a sitting position, the muscles in her arms, neck, and shoulders automatically lift the head up. A newborn who is sitting will attempt to lift her chin to raise her head. If the newborn infant is held in a standing position, her legs are usually limp at the hips and knees.

Senses: Your newborn baby can feel pain, sense the difference between hot and cold, recognize the voices he heard in the womb, and recognize the scent of his mother's breast milk.

Vision: Newborns can focus momentarily on a moving object that is positioned slightly above or slightly below their line of sight, and about 8 to 10 inches away.

Hearing: The baby is more likely to stop and listen to the sound of a human voice than to any other sound. Changes in heart rate and breathing rate indicate that the human voice has attracted the baby's attention.

Elimination: The average newborn urinates ten to fifteen times a day and also has frequent bowel movements—at least five a day after the first week of life.

Stimulation: Newborns are sensitive to changes in their environment. High levels of stimulation such as visual input can cause stress and affect infant behavior. The fragile, preterm infant is particularly vulnerable to combinations of stimuli such as noise, handling, and bright lights. Even social cues such as the parent's smiling face too close can cause distress in the premature baby.

Imitation: Between 60 and 70 percent of newborns can imitate tongue protrusion when demonstrated; 40 to 45 percent can imitate mouth opening.

Identification: Footprints and/or fingerprints may be taken at the hospital. Baby is usually weighed and measured.

The First Week Begins

DATE: _____

O

DAYS OLD

DATE: _____

I

DAY OLD

Just born! Welcome!

P Baby's blood is sampled right after birth and routinely screened for PKU, galactosemia, and hypothyroidism. All are inborn (but treatable) metabolic disorders. Babies from at-risk populations may also be screened for sickle-cell disease.

C Right after birth, babies tend to be quiet but alert for about half an hour. They can follow objects visually, stare, and make eye contact.

S Fussing, sucking or mouthing her hands, and "rooting" are all signs of hunger. When the baby "roots," she will automatically turn her head and open her mouth in search of food when her cheek is touched.

P Cutting the umbilical cord and sampling its blood are not painful for either the mom or her baby.

C Birth is an ordeal for the baby, too. The baby typically becomes fussy and sleepy but wakes up to feed every two to four hours.

S Breast-fed babies wake more often than bottle-fed ones. Breast milk is the perfect food and is so easily digested that breast-fed babies become hungry sooner than bottle-fed ones. (It's actually a good thing—very little waste.)

IMPORTANT Doctors strongly recommend putting baby to sleep on his side or his back, not on his stomach. The phrase "Back to Sleep" can be a reminder.

IMPORTANT Check your baby's birth certificate for accuracy.

Medical Consult your health-care provider to find out which commercial infant formulas are recommended as alternatives to breast-feeding.

Check This Out Other experienced women, your lactation consultant, and the La Leche League International (www.llli.org) are good resources for breast-feeding support.

KEY

P Physical Development

C Cognitive Development

S Social-Emotional Development

Nothing is worth more than this day.
J. W. GOETHE

2 DAYS OLD	DATE:

3 DAYS OLD	DATE:

(P) Baby's first bowel movements are normally tarry and greenish black because they contain meconium, the material that accumulated in the baby's bowel prior to birth. The color and consistency of the stools will change once your baby begins to drink breast milk.

(C) Babies communicate their needs by crying. In the beginning, cries are associated with the basics: hunger, fatigue, discomfort, and the need for physical contact. Everyone learns to decode their own baby's unique cries.

(S) It's difficult to interact with the baby since most of what she does is eat and sleep. But even now, baby's daily cycle involves periods of active alertness (interested looking) and quiet alertness (passive looking), when the two of you can study each other's faces.

(P) Your newborn's sneezing and coughing aren't usually signs of illness; instead, they are reflex reactions designed to clear amniotic fluid and mucous from your baby's airways to promote easier breathing.

(C) Evidence of an incredible form of early learning appears in the baby's ability to distinguish the characteristics of their most likely food source. Baby can begin to tell the difference between female voices and male ones, familiar voices and unfamiliar ones, and the smell of mother's skin. Even if babies are hardwired to notice voices in higher tone ranges (more likely belonging to women than men) and become familiar with voices they've heard, your baby still needs to be paying attention and actively processing auditory information. (Pretty amazing, huh?)

(S) You'll notice that the intensity of baby's crying sometimes goes from 0 to 60 mph in a matter of moments. (A Baby Maserati!) When your baby experiences stress—being too warm or hungry, for example—his blood sugar and fluid levels fluctuate wildly, because he is less able to process the fats, proteins, and carbohydrates in his diet. Once the endocrine system matures and glandular secretions regularize, baby should be better equipped to tolerate change.

IMPORTANT Your baby's lungs are brand new. Protect them by avoiding exposure to smoking, fumes, and pollution.

I have no name: I am but two days old. What shall I call thee?
I happy am, Joy is my name. Sweet joy befall thee!
WILLIAM BLAKE

Love Notes Especially in the months right before birth, your baby had skin-to-skin contact 24/7. She still needs the comfort of being held, especially against your bare chest. Being touched and held this way literally stimulates development and encourages weight gain by prompting the baby's body to manufacture and release the growth hormone. (So wear your baby early and often.)

Check This Out Think about calling in some favors from friends and relatives. Mothers of new babies—especially those with cesarean sections or other children at home—need help with just about everything.

Did You Know? Coughing, gagging, and short pauses in breathing are common as the baby's system becomes accustomed to inhaling air, not amniotic fluid.

notes

_____

_____

_____

_____

_____

_____

_____

_____

_____

_____

_____

_____

_____

_____

DATE:

4
DAYS OLD

Once the amniotic fluid has drained from their ears, infants probably have the auditory clarity of adults. Watch for a response when a bell is rung gently about 12 inches (30.5 cm) from baby's ear—a blink, frown, startle, increase in activity, or crying. Did she seem to hear it?

The sleep-wake pattern of the newborn during the first three days after birth is different from any sleep-wake pattern that occurred prenatally or any pattern established after three days of age. Apparently, the baby is adapting to the newness of life outside the womb. His sleep-wake cycle generally becomes more stabilized by today—Day 4.

By this time, most babies can recognize the primary caregiver's face (usually the mother) on the basis of visual cues alone. Babies seem to scan the eyes, hairline, chin, and the clothing that frames her face.

Having a baby is like trying to push a grand piano through a transom.

ALICE ROOSEVELT LONGWORTH

	DATE:
5 DAYS OLD	

	DATE:
6 DAYS OLD	

P If you're breast-feeding, baby's bowel movements may begin to look less black and more mustard yellow sometime within the next five days. Since breast milk has a laxative effect, your baby's stools are naturally loose, soft, and sometimes even watery. (And they don't smell! Check it out!)

C Watching your newborn's body language may help you be more responsive to your baby's needs. Squirming and/or grimacing may signal that baby is about to cry. When baby smacks his lips, he is usually looking for food.

S Babies are social creatures and now may begin to quiet when picked up. When babies are awake, they are usually happiest around the family. They can learn to nap in the more populated regions of the house by learning to tune out noise, just like older children and adults do. In addition, the baby is easier to check on since she is close by.

IMPORTANT Moms who breast-feed need to be as conscientious about their nutrient and fluid intake as they were during pregnancy, maybe even more so. A healthy diet continues to benefit baby directly and significantly. (And it's good for you, too!)

Love Notes Since newborns typically quiet to soft sounds, try using whispers, shushing, lullabies, and soft music to help them fall asleep. They also hear your heartbeat when held to your chest.

Did You Know? Breast-fed babies are less susceptible to diarrhea because substances in the breast milk seem to destroy the microorganisms that cause it. Until your milk comes in, baby is getting the nutritious pre-milk known as *colostrum*.

P Newborns are capable of detecting subtle smells. Babies as young as six hours old can distinguish the odor of their mother's breast milk from that of other nursing mothers. Even infants with no breast-feeding experience are attracted to the breast odor of a lactating woman over the smell of commercial formula.

C When you feed or hold your baby, let her study your face, hear your voice, and feel your touch. Your face is automatically in the best viewing position when you are breast- or bottle-feeding. When the baby is switched from one breast to the other and from one arm to the other from feeding to feeding, she gets a different view of her world.

S Don't expect a comfortable routine to develop quickly. Adjusting to the needs and patterns of a new baby requires trial-and-error problem solving. And, if this is a first child, everything changes; and that's almost always good. (You already knew the part about wanting sleep more than sex, right? Ah, sweet sleep!)

IMPORTANT Baby's crib needs to be safe. If two adult fingers can be placed between the mattress and the sides of the crib, the mattress is too small. If the sides of the crib have slats, they shouldn't be more than 2 inches (5 cm) apart.

People who say thay sleep like a baby usually don't have one.
LEO J. BURKE

7
DAYS OLD

DATE:

Did You Know? Smell is very primal. The newborn's sense of smell helps him identify his mother and find the food source.

The First Week ends

notes

P Any weight lost by your baby after birth (½ pound, or 227 grams, is common) will usually be regained by today or tomorrow. Weight is usually lost because of dehydration and nutrient loss during labor.

C Since birth, your baby's brain waves have been showing distinct patterns associated with active sleep, quiet or deep sleep, and waking. Unlike adults, the newborn cycles first into active sleep, followed by quiet or deep sleep. The pattern is repeated until waking. Research has confirmed what the body seems to know—that active sleep is a priority since it helps a new brain make developmental progress.

S The best time to interact with your baby is when she is alert, awake, and not distracted by hunger or other discomforts. Newborns are generally awake and quiet for two to three hours out of twenty-four, awake and active for one to two hours, asleep for sixteen to seventeen hours, and cry or fuss the remainder of the time.

Check This Out You'll probably notice more breast fullness during the next week as you and your baby become more adept at nursing. The more milk that is drained from the breasts, the more milk will be replaced, so baby has an adequate supply for each subsequent feeding.

Love Notes Rocking a baby is pure joy for everyone involved. But if you rock your baby during feeding, she may fall asleep before her hunger is completely satisfied. Thus, save rocking and other soothing activity for after feeding.

Babies are bits of star-dust blown from the hand of God.
Lucky the woman who knows the pangs of birth for she has held a star.
LARRY BARRETTO

8	DATE:
DAYS OLD	

9	DATE:
DAYS OLD	

The inborn need to suck is so strong that infants who are deprived of sucking, such as those with a cleft lip repair, may suck on their tongues. Some newborns are born with sucking pads on their fingers from sucking activity prior to birth. While nutritive sucking is (obviously) life sustaining, nonnutritive sucking of a thumb or a pacifier plays a critical role in self-soothing by decreasing crying and relieving distress.

The length of time week-old babies can remember a particular sound seems to be about one minute. Your baby will need to have a sound—like a ringing phone or a barking dog— repeated frequently to become familiar with it.

Newborns tend to show a visual preference for the human face, and babies as young as yours (just one week old) begin to watch people intently as they speak. As the newborn stares, her head may begin to bob up and down, and her mouth moves almost as if trying to say something. Newborns move their bodies in rhythm to human speech. This movement is called *interactional synchrony* or the *language dance*. This movement suggests that infants are born with the ability to recognize the sound of human speech. (That works!)

The soft spot, or fontanel, on the top of your baby's skull isn't as tender as you might think. Although his head should be protected from getting bumped, and baby should never be in danger of falling, you can clean this spot as you do the rest of the scalp when you wash baby's hair—with gentle soap, rubbing, and rinsing.

Eighty-four percent of babies in their first two weeks of life tend to cry when exposed to the sound of another crying infant—a behavior called *imitative crying*. This is not just a tendency to cry in response to a loud or noxious sound, as demonstrated by the fact that newborns cry more when exposed to the cries of other newborns than they do to the cries of older infants, noise that sounds like crying, the cries of a chimpanzee, or silence. This behavior might reveal the earliest hint of empathy or the ability to feel the distress of another.

There's something really wonderful about the way that babies smell, especially their heads. Check it out. Hold baby upright against your chest and inhale deeply. It's that new-baby smell! And our reaction is probably adaptive—if we are attracted to the way babies smell, we're probably more inclined to care for them and keep them *close*. (And that keeps everybody in the gene pool for at least one more day!)

IMPORTANT Attend all of your baby's scheduled well-child visits with the doctor. Your baby will receive checkups, and you can discuss the pros and cons of immunization and other practices with your health-care provider. The first visit usually takes place when the baby is around two weeks old.

The three most beautiful sights: a potato garden in bloom, a ship in sail, and a woman after the birth of her child.

IRISH PROVERB

10 DAYS OLD

DATE:

11 DAYS OLD

DATE:

Ⓟ If your baby boy was circumcised, his penis should heal in seven to fourteen days. If there's irritation or you have questions, contact your health-care provider.

Ⓒ Newborns tend to respond to loud sounds by startling or crying. Because hearing plays such a critical role in language learning and social interaction, baby's hearing is tested before leaving the hospital or birthing center.

Ⓢ If you plan to share caregiving tasks with another person—your partner, a relative, or a daycare provider—it would be ideal if she was involved with the baby from the beginning. If such involvement is not practical or possible, ease the baby's transition by spending time together as a trio and letting baby receive care from this person in your presence. At this age, your baby probably won't object to the other person or protest your absence, but she can be expected to show—by changes in her behavior—that she has noticed that something's different.

Ⓟ You may notice your baby's skin beginning to peel during these first few weeks, often starting with her fingers and toes. This exfoliation is natural—no scrubbing or peeling is necessary— and makes way for a new layer of healthy skin.

Ⓒ Even at this young age, your baby may turn his head toward a noise, especially if that noise is high-pitched like a female voice.

Ⓢ By Day 10 or 11, enough regular interactions have taken place between infant and caregiver that the baby will probably notice any shifts in routine. In this relatively brief time frame, the baby has already recognized a pattern in the primary caregiver's style and become accustomed to it. (Amazing!)

IMPORTANT If you bottle-feed, keep the bottles, nipples, and any internal components very clean. After feeding, throw away any formula left in the bottle, wash it with warm sudsy water, and rinse it thoroughly.

Did You Know? Most babies lose 5 to 10 percent of their birth weight because of the rigors of being born. By the time of your baby's first checkup, she should be back to birth weight or heavier.

Medical Do you feel sad or depressed? Do you cry or feel like crying? If you feel overwhelmed or out of your element for most of the day, day after day, you may want to contact your health-care provider. As debilitating and unpleasant as these feelings are, they are also quite common and treatable if they persist.

Which is the way to Baby-Land? Any one can tell; Up one flight, To your right; Please to ring the bell.

GEORGE COOPER

<table>
<tr><td>1 2
DAYS OLD</td><td>DATE:</td></tr>
</table>

Cephalocaudal is a type of development pattern that babies are guided by; it progresses from the head downward. Predictably then, head control is one of baby's first challenges. Major progress is made by Day 30, when most babies are able to hold their big, heavy heads erect for three seconds or more. The comparable achievement for an adult would be to balance a head that is 8 cubic feet (2 feet by 2 feet by 2 feet, or .2 cubic meters) in volume instead of his or her existing one, the volume of which is a little less than 1 cubic foot (1 foot by 1 foot by 1 foot, or .03 cubic meters). (Trade in those turtleneck sweaters for helmets!)

The idea of play is an interesting one. It's something that is done for fun or pleasure. Researchers regard play as the child's work.

A prompt, caring response to your baby's crying is best. It makes infants feel secure by letting them know that they can depend on the people around them to take care of their needs. Rather than spoiling babies, responding promptly actually encourages babies to cry less. (Sweet!)

<table>
<tr><td>1 3
DAYS OLD</td><td>DATE:</td></tr>
</table>

Your newborn may begin to make some movements with his head as soon as he's three days old (more than a week ago). When lying face down on a firm surface, the baby may make movements to free his nose by turning his head to the side or by lifting it free of the surface.

It is important to talk to your baby when you feed, change, bathe, or play with her and listen when she makes sounds. Your baby may begin to respond to you by smiling and squealing as you talk to her. These activities promote language development and facilitate bonding.

After you pick baby up to encourage him to stop crying, place him in a high, shoulder-to-front position. This position has been found to be the most effective about 85 percent of the time. (Here's hoping you're not in that latter 15 percent!)

IMPORTANT Be sure to check the temperature of your baby's bathwater by dipping your elbow in the water. Bathwater should feel warm, not hot.

Did You Know? Research confirms that picking up a baby is the most effective method of getting her to stop crying for the time being.

A baby is the most complicated object made by unskilled labor.

ANONYMOUS

14
DAYS OLD

DATE:

notes

P Effort in your baby's head control can be observed when she is being held upright against your shoulder. Move your hand slowly down from supporting her head to supporting her back. She should be able to lift her head off your shoulder intermittently.

C Your baby may give a bright toy (like a red ring) a momentary glance. In another two weeks, her attention span should double, even triple, in length—a bright object should catch her attention for several seconds before she looks away.

S Reflex smiling (compared to social smiling) is noticed most often during sleep, when baby's mouth pulls back at the corners and only the muscles of the lower face are involved.

Week 2 ends

There was never a child so lovely but his mother was glad to get him asleep.

RALPH WALDO EMERSON

15 DAYS OLD	DATE:	16 DAYS OLD	DATE:

P The firmness and color of your baby's skin can provide important clues about his general health. Contact your health-care provider if your baby's skin looks grayish or yellowish.

C Some of the baby's earliest mental challenges involve telling the difference between familiar experiences and unfamiliar ones. The memory that supports this kind of discrimination is developing right now.

S Social smiles are voluntary smiles in response to people and objects. Social smiling—in people of all ages—involves smiling with the corners of the eyes, too. (So, is the smile you see polite or heartfelt? Become a smile-watcher ☺. You'll learn a lot.)

Medical Your baby's first checkup (usually scheduled around two weeks of age) is primarily designed to make sure baby is feeding well, growing well, healing well, sleeping adequately, and gaining weight. Caregivers are encouraged to bring all of their questions and concerns to the appointment.

Love Notes One of the most wonderful consequences of baby's poor head control at your shoulder is feeling your baby's head bump into your cheek to stabilize itself. What exquisite contact, but how short-lived the pleasure! Development marches on!

P The rooting reflex of a breast-fed infant is generally better developed than that of a bottle-fed baby. The breast-fed baby has to actively search for the nipple; for the bottle-fed baby, rooting is unnecessary. You'll most likely see the reflex in action when the baby is hungry or drowsy. Placing the baby in her regular feeding position also cues the rooting reflex.

C Laughter and baby sounds rank among the most delightful things humans are privileged to hear. The Navajo of the American Southwest understand this well. In tribal tradition, when a Navajo infant laughs for the first time, the members of the tribe exchange gifts to mark the occasion. The person who makes the baby laugh hosts the party!

S Swaddling often quiets very young infants. It involves restraining baby's limbs by wrapping him snugly in a light blanket. (Voilà! A burrito baby!)

The heart is the toughest part of the body. Tenderness is in the hands.
CAROLYN FORCHE

1 7	DATE:
DAYS OLD	

1 8	DATE:
DAYS OLD	

Ⓟ At birth, all of your baby's senses are functional. Touch, smell, and hearing are the most well developed; taste provides very basic information; and vision is the least well developed. Even early on, the infant's system is able to organize and integrate information from more than one sense. For example, your baby may turn her head to visually search for a sound that she hears. In this way, one sensory system supports another as your baby learns about her world.

Ⓒ Even though babies don't know what they're tasting and/or smelling, they react strongly to pleasant and unpleasant sensations. If baby has a bite of lemon, he might shudder, make a sour face, and jettison his tongue from his mouth. If he smells something powerful like ammonia, he might recoil and turn his head away.

Ⓢ A baby who is crying because she's hungry can be quieted only temporarily by soothing strategies. Babies differ greatly in how soothable they are by any strategy and how agitated they become when they want to be fed.

Did You Know? Your child's ability to focus attention is a seminal skill. Sustained attention is required for reading comprehension, language acquisition, social interaction, skill building, and memory function.

Love Notes Part of loving a baby is understanding why she is so impatient to be fed, changed, or held. At this point in her life, she simply can't wait, because her nervous system is too immature to temper her own reactions. Her patience develops with time and maturity—and so does ours.

Ⓟ Sometime within the first month, your baby may begin to display an alerting response, for instance, to the sound of a rattle. Your baby may stop what he's doing and appear to listen. If the sound is repeated several times, the baby responds to it less and less. This behavior demonstrates that baby notices the sound and then recognizes that that sound is no longer new, but repeated. This type of learning is called *habituation*. All of us habituate all the time.

Ⓒ By the time your baby was two to four days old, she was already able to indicate a preference for the less bright of two lights, regardless of their color. She still prefers light that is less intense.

Ⓢ Your baby is expanding his vocal repertoire to include small throaty sounds like "ah" and "uh," coos, gurgles, sighs, grunts, squeals, and bubbles. Once he can do more than cry, you can actively try to elicit some kind of noise from him and begin to have a "conversation."

notes

_____

_____

_____

_____

_____

_____

_____

_____

The beginning is the most important part of the work.

PLATO

19 DAYS OLD

DATE:

P Your baby was born with two reflexes that help protect her vision. The baby's pupil automatically adjusts to light intensity by narrowing in bright light and widening in dim light (a reaction called the *pupillary reflex*). She also automatically blinks or closes her eyes when an object comes too close or is too bright for her pupil to handle effectively. In this way, the outside of the eye is protected by the eyelid, while the delicate cells on the inside are shielded by the pupil.

C Sharp, loud sounds can cause a baby as young as three days old to stop what she is doing and listen. (This reflex is probably a protective response—a loud sound might indicate danger—and one that doesn't disappear with age.)

S Newborns are highly touch sensitive. Since they have less skin surface than someone older, their skin receptors are more concentrated, particularly around the mouth and hands. When touched, newborns show changes in heart rate.

Did You Know? When physical, cognitive, or social development is under way in a child age six or younger, weight gain is essential to healthy functioning and is considered a normal and desirable sign of good nutrition. The amount and disposition of gained weight is an important consideration, however, even in very young children.

Love Notes Human physical contact forms the foundation for emotional attachment. The attachment of the parent to the baby and vice versa probably begins before birth and is strengthened when the parent holds and cuddles the baby.

notes

A healthy newborn has been delivered in a more or less satisfying fashion. The baby is feeding well, has short nails and a clean bottom, and has not drowned. What now?

SANDRA SCARR

2 0 DAYS OLD   DATE:

2 1 DAYS OLD   DATE:

For all babies, the kind of balance that permits sitting and standing begins with head control. Sometime between days 3 and 30, your baby may begin to make lateral head movements (using a side-to-side motion to balance her head). Baby may be able to lift her head when held at the shoulder and hold it erect for three seconds.

Babies can see objects most clearly if the image is 8 to 10 inches (20 to 25 cm) from baby's face as he lies on his back. Movement helps attract attention, but it's momentary.

Newborns can distinguish facial expressions of emotion that include happy, sad, and surprised. Being able to acknowledge these different facial expressions is the first step in understanding the feelings they convey.

Crying for no apparent reason increases during these first few months from a daily total of one to one and a half hours by three weeks, building to two to four hours by six weeks. This unprovoked crying may be related to the discharge of energy and maturational changes in the baby's brain. Baby seems to settle down by Week 12, and so will you.

Learning depends on pattern recognition, and pattern recognition depends on memory and experience. Early learning involves noticing that two events are associated with each other, like seeing the nipple and getting fed.

Babies cue off other people's emotions just like adults do. Furthermore, our emotions tinge our actions. Even a young baby senses stress and negativity on the faces and through the actions of his caregivers. If your sadness and pain don't resolve in a reasonable amount of time, consider getting help.

Check This Out It's never too early to interest children in books and to take a trip to the local bookstore or library. Hold baby while you look through a picture book or magazine. Reading and understanding what is read is the single most important skill for school success. (Actually, the *ability* to show up for school is more important, but you know what I mean.)

Week 3 ends

Little children disturb your sleep, big ones your life.
YIDDISH PROVERB

DATE:

DATE:

(P) By about one month of age, the bottle-fed baby has usually practiced sucking long enough to suck more efficiently with less sputtering and choking. Breast-fed babies have to work harder to get the breast to release milk, so they don't choke or sputter much, if ever.

(C) During this first month, your baby's hearing is sophisticated enough to perceive a difference between the ringing of a bell and the sound of a rattle. Thus, environmental sounds are more than just "noise" to the young infant.

(S) Most of adult memory is related to language. For example, what's the name of your first boyfriend or girlfriend? Infant memory is more like a photo album without captions.

(P) By three weeks of age, the rooting reflex associated with feeding has probably disappeared or developed into voluntary head-turning. Voluntary head-turning involves a single, well-aimed head movement that brings your baby's mouth into contact with the nipple.

(C) Your baby can probably follow a moving object at eye level in front of him in a range of about 90 degrees—that's less than half his visual field (about one quarter of a circle).

(S) Tactile stimulation is essential for baby's optimum growth and development. Tactile activities include holding, caressing, and cuddling your baby; pushing her hair aside; tracing her features; and holding and studying her hands. Most infants enjoy being held, walked, bounced, patted, and rocked.

Love Notes Keep your baby comfortably warm and wrap her snugly when you interact. Hold her firmly, hug her tenderly, kiss her cheeks, and stroke her hair. Memorize what she looks and feels like at this exact moment so you can keep the image in your mind forever.

A sparkling house is a fine thing if the children aren't robbed of their luster by keeping it that way.
MARCELENE COX

	DATE:
24 DAYS OLD	

	DATE:
25 DAYS OLD	

Ⓟ Your baby's tear glands will begin to function by today, if not sooner. Prior to this time, his eyes may have gotten watery, but no tears would flow.

Ⓒ During the first month of life, your baby begins to adapt her reflexes to match the demands of the environment. For example, the sucking reflex, which is vital to feeding, is highly adaptable to such features as the size of the object placed in the mouth, the object's position, whether it's edible, and its temperature (within a reasonable range). Some consider this ability to convert reflexes into voluntary actions to be the beginning of cognition or the baby's ability to think and solve problems.

Ⓢ When you lift your baby to your shoulder, you may notice that he is able to hold his head more erect than before.

Ⓟ Your baby's head circumference increases by about ½ inch (1.27 cm) this month as her brain grows rapidly. (Good thing those baby headbands are made to stretch!)

Ⓒ Your baby uses inborn reflexes, like grasping, smiling, and sucking, to experience the world. While baby isn't yet able to plan an action and carry it out, he is able to gather information about objects and people by responses. For example, your baby's fingers automatically grasp anything placed in the palm of his hand—clothing, a toy, a strand of hair—giving him the opportunity to feel different textures and, in time, to look at what was grasped.

Ⓢ Speak to your baby often, no matter what you are doing. She can watch you intently and enjoy the interaction while growing more familiar with what will become her native language.

Did You Know? The automatic reflex behaviors that your baby was born with will be gradually replaced by voluntary patterns of behavior. In that way, she is less controlled by her environment and more in control of what she does and when she does it.

Behold the child, by Nature's kindly law, pleased with a rattle, tickled with a straw.

ALEXANDER POPE

26
DAYS OLD

DATE:

(P) The average length of the longest sleep period for babies as old as yours (three to four weeks of age) is about three and a half hours. Your own baby may sleep longer or shorter than the average.

(C) Infants younger than one month of age look at objects and people and hear sounds but are just beginning to relate the sounds to a particular person or thing. If you interact frequently with your baby, he begins to associate your voice with your face, but connecting a dog with a bark or a rattle sound with a toy is going to take more maturity and practice.

(S) Baby's increased smiling in response to the sights and sounds of her parents and others helps parents connect with their infants as baby humans and develop an interest in them.

27
DAYS OLD

DATE:

(P) Your baby's back and head continue to form one complete curve when she is held in a sitting position.

(C) Provide something for baby's senses and muscles to do in the form of basic and brief opportunities to look, listen, and touch. These experiences help baby's sensory and motor systems organize and get ready for learning.

(S) With increasing frequency, your baby will begin to glance at you or notice your movements when you talk to him to attract his attention.

Check This Out See how successful you can be at encouraging your baby to gurgle or make movements when you speak to her.

Week 4 ends

notes

From what we get, we can make a living; what one gives, however, makes a life.
ARTHUR ASHE

28 DAYS OLD	DATE:

29 DAYS OLD	DATE:

(P) The physical growth rate following birth is unparalleled during infancy. In four short weeks, your baby is expected to grow about 1 inch (2.5 cm) in length and add 4 to 6 ounces (113 to 170 g) to her weight each week! A 5-foot (1.5-m), 100-pound (45-kg) adult who grew at this rate would measure a full 6 feet (1.8 m) and weigh 120 pounds (54 kg) by the end of a year's time!

(C) When babies start to follow moving objects with their eyes, it is easier for them to begin to track objects moving horizontally (right to left or left to right). So, if you want your baby to look at an object, place it in the middle of his visual field and move it from side to side rather than up and down. Horizontal tracking will be well established by two months of age.

(S) By the end of the first month, the combination of visual and auditory stimuli is more effective than an auditory stimulus alone in eliciting active smiling, now displayed as a grin. Interactive fun, like patty-cake and eensy weensy spider, contains elements that might provoke a smile. Even more significant, they involve skin-to-skin touch, so baby's not just having fun, she is having fun with someone she's falling in love with!

(P) Some babies may develop blemishes or acne on their skin. The acne may be triggered by maternal hormones that are still in baby's system or be due to underdeveloped pores. Infant complexion problems need no special attention; these signs are not precursors of later skin problems.

(C) Young babies are very near-sighted (no real distance vision yet). While something interesting might be across the room or just a few feet away, your baby won't be able to appreciate it until his vision markedly improves.

(S) By about this time, your baby should become calm to the sound of a nearby soothing human voice. However, your infant won't quiet if she is hungry and wants to be fed.

Did You Know? Just how nearsighted are month-old infants? A baby's visual acuity ranges from 20/100 to 20/600, while 20/20 is standard vision for adults. Thus, a baby must sit 20 inches (51 cm) from an object to see what a person with standard vision can see at a distance of 100 to 600 inches (254 to 1,524 cm).

Love Notes Look at your baby and see how much he has changed in just four short weeks and how his characteristics are beginning to resemble—or not—members of the family.

After your baby arrives, you yourself may feel like something of a present, albeit clumsy, wrapped in unmatched ribbons and bows, but new. Untried. Untested.

SALLY PLACKSIN

30 DAYS OLD	DATE:

31 DAYS OLD	DATE:

Ⓟ Due to practice and maturation, you can expect baby to turn her head immediately to the side when placed on her stomach, flex her arms and legs, and hunch up her buttocks in the fetal position. She may also be able to lift her head momentarily.

Ⓒ Learning associations between two events teaches your baby to anticipate certain outcomes. For example, he might learn to anticipate being lifted up when you bend down and extend your arms with your palms exposed. This type of learning is called *classical conditioning.*

Ⓢ While parents are the architects of their baby's environment, they are also the regulators. Watch for signs that your baby has had enough of the activities she's involved in: fussiness, restlessness, or inattention. Even young infants can get overstimulated and overwhelmed by too much for too long. (Think about how you feel in a crowded airport with a flight delay and no place to sit down.)

Ⓟ Around the beginning of baby's second month, infants are feeding six to seven times a day and drinking about 3.2 ounces (91 ml) per feeding. A breast-fed baby continues to take what is needed at each feeding. Your baby's feeding habits will probably vary around these averages to a greater or lesser extent.

Ⓒ At one month of age, your baby can't reach and grasp or let go of an object voluntarily. Consequently, anything placed in baby's hand (like a rattle) might be dropped almost immediately or grasped tenaciously.

Ⓢ As early as three days after birth, your baby may have tried to make eye contact with you or another person. Now that he's a month old, he may temporarily interrupt his activity when he sees you in order to make eye contact. Ceasing activity when he sees you may indicate that he is beginning to anticipate that your presence might foreshadow some interaction, such as lifting, feeding, changing, or transporting.

IMPORTANT Overstimulation is a special concern for the premature baby, who is even more sensitive to sensory overload than the full-term infant. Less is actually just the right amount for the baby who was premature.

Did You Know? Physically, a woman's body needs from one to two years to fully recover from pregnancy. This recovery time allows siblings to be spaced two to three years apart.

Sufficient unto the day is one baby. As long as you are in your right mind, don't you ever pray for twins. Twins amount to a permanent riot; and there ain't any real difference between triplets and an insurrection.

MARK TWAIN

32 DAYS OLD   DATE:

33 DAYS OLD   DATE:

P   Although you may have ideas about foods you think your baby might like, most of her digestive processes do not begin to function until Week 12. That's why most pediatricians recommend no solid food for babies under four months of age.

C   Most babies like to look at mobiles. Mobiles give babies practice perceiving depth, form, color, and movement.

S   Sometime between the first and third months, infants begin to vocalize in response to the vocalizations of others. Baby won't necessarily repeat the same sounds, but he may engage in exchanges of ten to fifteen vocalizations. This early form of dialogue is another important sign that baby is developing social responsiveness.

notes

P   Baby's first immunizations are typically given sometime between birth and two months of age. The Hpb or HepB vaccine protects baby against hepatitis B viral infection. The virus does serious damage to the liver, which screens out toxins from the blood.

C   When your baby is older and more active, she may learn that she can make a mobile move by shaking the sides of her crib or jumping up and down. (The mobile mobile!)

S   After the first month, crying seems almost obligatory for a baby. A crying infant may stop crying to smile at an interesting toy and then resume crying again when the toy is taken away.

Medical Discuss the need for and safety of the HepB vaccine for your child with his pediatrician.

Did You Know? When a month-old baby is placed on his back, he assumes a more elongated posture than he did as a newborn—his limbs are straighter and his knees are farther apart. "Finally," baby says, "leg room!"

. . . what gives mother love its difficulty and its grandeur is the fact that it implies no reciprocity.

SIMONE DE BEAUVOIR

	DATE:
34 DAYS OLD	

P Your baby's back still may be rounded like a "C" when she is seated. Sitting with support (on someone's lap or against furniture) is generally well established between months 2 and 4.

C Baby should be able to visually track a bright, moving object or person for a few seconds. Tracking movement side to side is usually established before up-down tracking.

S Because your baby probably wiggles a lot, he can roll off any raised surface. Never leave your baby unattended or turn your back on him even for a moment.

notes

	DATE:
35 DAYS OLD	

P During the first five weeks, wakefulness during the day tends to increase, but the amount of wakefulness during the night does not. (Yes!)

C When faced with looming objects, one- to two-month-old babies may make more backward head movements than when confronted with nonlooming objects. This reaction indicates the beginning of distance and depth perception (see below).

S Sometime between month 1 and 2, baby may begin to respond to her primary caregiver when the adult bends to change a diaper, for example, and talks to her. Any smiling or intense gazing seems to indicate recognition.

IMPORTANT Few things are as important as actively supervising your baby. It's easy to underestimate the speed, reach, and strength of these little ones. Your supervision can make a literal life-or-death difference.

Check This Out A looming object is something that comes closer and closer, as if it is going to hit the observer. An example of a looming object would be your hand moving forward, palm up, in an exaggerated "stop" movement. You can observe your baby's reaction to your looming hand or a looming object held in your hand.

Week 5 ends

Yes, having a child is surely the most beautifully irrational act that two people in love can commit.
BILL COSBY

36
DAYS OLD

DATE:

37
DAYS OLD

DATE:

P For the first two months or so, your baby may require at least two night feedings. By around three months of age, just one feeding at night becomes more typical.

C Circular eye coordination allows baby's eyes to follow a brightly colored object moving in a circle about 12 inches (30 cm) in diameter above his eyes. The baby's eyes should follow some of the circular movement in the upper and lower halves of the circle, but his eyes are not expected to follow in one continuous circle quite yet.

S The baby's vocalizations are so delightful, but it's not all play and no work. Your baby is beginning to produce syllable sounds that vary slightly from each other. Listen carefully for the differences between sounds—like "gah" and "guh."

P Sometime between one and one and a half months of age, your baby may be able to roll partway to her side when placed on her stomach.

C Listen to the sounds baby makes when he is vocalizing freely. In addition to some syllable sounds, you may be able to identify at least two distinct and separate vowel sounds like "ay," "ah," "uh," "ooh," "eeh," or "eh."

S Whether they are vowels or syllables or just noise, your baby has about four times as much to say as she did during her first month. That makes perfect sense—she's nearly twice as old as she was then!

Medical The pertussis (whooping cough) vaccine is part of the vaccination protocol for infants. Whooping cough is a highly contagious disease that can make infants seriously ill. Discuss the need for and safety of the DTaP vaccine for your child with her pediatrician.

Check This Out So what color are your baby's eyes? They may seem one color now, but . . . it's actually too soon to tell.

A couple's relationship often moves to the back burner as they focus on the new baby and temporarily prefer sleep over sex.

SUSAN LAPINSKI

38 DAYS OLD	DATE:

39 DAYS OLD	DATE:

ⓟ The DTaP vaccine also protects against diptheria and tetanus, both of which produce toxins and can make babies seriously ill. Discuss the need for and safety of this vaccine with your pediatrician.

ⓒ You can make your baby's world more interesting by offering her animated objects to look at and toys that make sounds or play music.

ⓢ By two months of age, your baby may begin to show signs of attachment to the person who functions as the secondary caregiver, if that person interacts with her regularly and positively.

ⓟ The HIB inoculation targets the microorganism that causes inflammation of the membranes that enclose your baby's brain and spinal cord. Discuss the need for and safety of this vaccine with your pediatrician.

ⓒ *Binocularity* is the ability of the brain to blend the image from each eye into a single picture of the world. Binocularity may begin to develop by six weeks and is usually well established by four months.

ⓢ Want to get a smile from your baby? Try smiling, touching or tickling, talking, nodding, and/or leaning close to him.

Love Notes These are the rewards babies can offer loving, responsive parenting: smiling, intense looking, increased activity, rapid breathing, vocalizing, and a brightening facial expression. Priceless!

notes

_____

_____

_____

_____

_____

_____

_____

_____

_____

_____

_____

_____

_____

If only we could have them back as babies today, now that we have some idea what to do with them.
NANCY MAIRS

40 DAYS OLD	DATE:

P Polio is a disease that attacks the brain and spinal cord, destroying tissue and resulting in muscular weakness and paralysis. IPOL vaccinates against all known forms of polio.

C The vocalizations heard during crying and vocal play eventually become syllables and then words. For example, "mama" or "nana" heard during vigorous crying may become the word that refers to the primary caregiver. (Ooh. That would be so nice! Please make it so.)

S Anticipating when your baby is getting sleepy and how long he will likely sleep is an art. Does the data give us a little help? Not much. Half of babies the age of yours sleep less than fifteen hours per day and half sleep more. Half of babies like yours sleep more than seven times a day and half sleep less. One thing's for sure—your baby's somewhere in that mix!

41 DAYS OLD	DATE:

P Sometime between weeks 4 and 8, your baby may begin to sit without support. Prop her in a sitting position on your lap using both of your hands, then gradually release your supportive hold. She may tense her muscles in an effort to remain seated.

C Sometime between weeks 4 and 6, baby should begin to turn his eyes and head toward light. The light attracts the baby's visual attention because it looks distinct from its surroundings and because the brain is practicing holding that attention span for a few seconds.

S During this time, dynamic movement— nodding your head, flicking the lights on and off, or coming into baby's line of sight—may provoke active smiling, cooing, and grinning.

Medical Don't give your baby any medicine without consulting your health-care provider first.

The key to everything is patience. You get the chicken by hatching the egg, not by smashing it.
ARNOLD H. GLASOW

42
DAYS OLD

DATE:

Convergence, or the ability of both eyes to work together to see close objects clearly, begins to develop around this time and is usually well established by three months.

Your baby's tendency to respond to a voice is usually well established by one month of age; her sensitivity to the source of other sounds begins to sharpen between now and Week 15.

By six weeks of age your baby may show more interest in a picture of a human face with eyes than a picture of a face without eyes. This reaction probably indicates that your baby has studied the features of the human face enough to know that the eyes are an essential component. The opportunity to make eye contact seems important even to a young infant.

Week 6 ends

To heir is human.

DOLORES E. MCGUIRE

43
DAYS OLD

DATE:

44
DAYS OLD

DATE:

When the eyes converge, they turn in slightly toward the nose. It's the angle of the eyes working together that the baby's brain has to learn to control.

Sometime between three and nine weeks, your baby should begin to move his eyes in an apparent effort to search for the sound he hears. Put baby in his crib, stand at the head of the crib out of his direct line of vision, and ring a bell first at one side and then at the other. There may not be any definite head movement toward the sound until two to four months, but your baby's eyes may move slowly from side to side in search of the sound.

More and more you may notice that your baby smiles when spoken to and is soothed by her mother's voice.

Did You Know? How interesting that such a fundamental point of human connection—looking another person in the eye—would be established by the time the baby is only a month and a half old!

Check This Out Play this game with your baby: Hold a rattle or a bell 8 to 10 inches (20 to 25 cm) from the baby's ear and shake it briefly; she may turn her head toward the source of the sound. (Let her see the rattle or bell briefly when she turns toward it before shaking it opposite the other ear.)

Sometime between one and two months of age, your baby's abs are strong enough to execute a leg lift lasting for at least two seconds while he is lying on his back!

Visual acuity is the ability to see clearly and accurately. It develops rapidly during baby's first six months of life but particularly during this second month.

You and your baby may spend the first three months or so establishing some pattern of feeding, sleeping, and wakeful activity. While some of your baby's rhythms are similar to those experienced before birth, caregivers usually try to lengthen periods of sleep, especially during the night hours. (C'mon little one, give us a break!)

Adam and Eve had many advantages, but the principal one was that they escaped teething.
MARK TWAIN

| 45 DAYS OLD | DATE: | 46 DAYS OLD | DATE: |

In about a week (at two months or so), your baby may be able to thrust her arms and legs when lying on her side or back. Leg and arm thrusts in different positions demonstrate baby's increasing ability to move her muscles.

For babies the age of yours, visual acuity is somewhere between 20/300 and 20/800. This means baby must be placed within 20 inches (51 cm) of an object to see what a person with 20/20 vision can see at a distance of 300 to 800 inches (762 to 2,032 cm).

By six to eight weeks, your baby may begin to smile in response to seeing something or someone he likes. This *social smile* has a profound effect on family members who now prolong their interactions with baby in the hopes of saying or doing something—anything!—that can bring on that delightful smile.

Love Notes The day your baby smiles and vocalizes to you just because you're there easily qualifies as a peak parenting experience!

Leg and arm thrusts in different positions also help develop your baby's range of motion. (Hi-ya!)

The first environmental sounds that baby seems to notice are sharp, loud sounds. Between days 3 and 30, he may have stopped his movement to listen to the sound of a bell or rattle. Now, sometime between three and eight weeks of age, baby seems primed to listen for human sounds.

Another fundamental element of human connection is well established by now—the tendency to respond to the sound of a human voice. Even if she does not see a person, when the baby hears a voice, she may turn her head, vocalize, stop any activity, change her facial expression, or give some other indication of attention and listening. Fascinating!

Diaper spelled backwards spells r-e-p-a-i-d. Think about it.

MARSHALL MCLUHAN

47
DAYS OLD

DATE:

48
DAYS OLD

DATE:

49
DAYS OLD

DATE:

It's another big month for brain growth. Baby's head circumference will increase by about ½ inch (1.27 cm) this month.

By this time, your baby's visual preferences have broadened to include not only high contrast, sharpness, and brightness, but complexity. Babies look longer at items with many elements than with few. (Time to bring out your sponge collection.)

In the first year, a baby is thought to develop a sense of trust or mistrust for his caregivers based on daily interactions. Trust is more likely if his needs are met in a timely way; mistrust becomes more likely if baby is ignored or mistreated.

Your baby's fine motor, or small-muscle, development allows her to have her hands open more often. An open hand makes exploration by touch more effective.

By two months, infants seem to discriminate between intact faces and faces with scrambled or absent features. (Make sure your nose stays where it's supposed to be.)

Play during infancy revolves primarily around a baby's own body—babies watch their hands, suck their fingers, and vocalize before becoming more sophisticated and interactive.

Sometime between 2 and 4 weeks, a baby placed on his stomach may begin to elevate himself, lifting his head and shoulders from the surface by pushing with his arms, elbows, or hands. It will take until four months of age, however, to perfect that voluntary push-up. (Is there a personal trainer in the house?)

Face perception plays an important role in social interaction and also confirms the baby's ability to match one item to another from memory.

Pleasure during play is demonstrated by quieting in the first month, followed by smiling (this month), and then by squealing (sometime during the third month).

Did You Know? Having hands open more frequently and the fading of the grasp reflex are two signs that fine motor development is probably progressing well.

Week 7 ends

notes

_____

_____

_____

_____

_____

_____

_____

The happiest days are when the babies come.
MARGARET MITCHELL

50 DAYS OLD   DATE:

51 DAYS OLD   DATE:

(P) Most babies the age of yours can grasp and shake toys, stretch and kick their legs, and begin to bring their hands to their mouth. (Watch out world! Here she comes!)

(C) By this time, most babies can distinguish their mother's face from that of a female stranger.

(S) Even so, your baby isn't ready for a face-to-face conversation quite yet. He can usually hold his head up when seated, but his back still needs support, and his head generally bobs forward.

(P) By about this time (two months of age), the cartilage in the soft spot toward the fontanel has usually hardened into bone.

(C) Sometime between one and three months old, baby may begin to coordinate reaching, grasping, and manipulating objects by hand.

(S) Try this: Suspend a red ring (or other brightly colored object) above your baby but within easy reach. If he is looking at the ring, he may move his arms in its direction even though the movements are still rather uncoordinated. This marks the beginning of *eye-hand coordination.*

Check This Out When will the frontal fontanel close? The soft spot in the middle of the skull above baby's forehead will probably close between eighteen and twenty-four months.

BABY POWDER

Sometimes you gotta create what you want to be a part of.
GERI WEITZMAN

5 2 DAYS OLD	DATE:

P Between now and week 15, babies tend to average less than fifteen hours of sleep per day, and most have a predictable nap schedule.

C Young infants get tired of seeing the same mobile, picture book, or toy. Renew the items in baby's line of sight frequently to include patterns of all types in medium-intensity colors and contrasts. (There are great baby books at your local library.)

S By about two months of age, your baby may vocalize vowel sounds called coos when playing alone or when she's talked to. (It makes you wonder what's going through her head, doesn't it?)

notes

_____
_____
_____
_____
_____
_____
_____
_____
_____
_____
_____
_____
_____

5 3 DAYS OLD	DATE:

P Your baby may begin to turn from his side onto his back. Play this game: In his crib, when he's unrestricted by clothing, roll him from his back onto his side. Make sure his arm is not caught beneath him, and flex one or both knees to prevent passive rolling. His muscles will flex if he actively turns from his side onto his back.

C Sometime between one and three months of age, your baby may begin to turn her head (instead of her entire body) to follow a moving object.

S Try this: Hold a brightly colored ball out 8 to 10 inches (20 to 25 cm) above his eyes with your right hand and a piece of paper in your left hand. Attract the baby's attention to the ball and then move it slowly (1 inch per second) in a horizontal direction until it passes behind the paper. Did he follow the moving ball with his body or his eyes? (Don't worry if he didn't—it's still early for this kind of visual tracking.)

Did You Know? Your baby's ability to produce vocalizations that are distinct from crying marks a major milestone in the development of speech.

Check This Out Some babies fall into a predictable daily sleep pattern as early as week 3. So what's up with your baby if he's less than predictable? Nothing, it's just individual variation.

A baby is born with a need to be loved and never outgrows it.

FRANK A. CLARK

54 DAYS OLD	DATE:

55 DAYS OLD	DATE:

The growth rate of your baby's brain is still astounding. At birth, it weighed about 25 percent of it's future adult size; by six months it may weigh 50 percent as much as the brain of an adult.

Visually tracking horizontal movement generally develops before the tracking of vertical movement, probably because of the way the eyes are situated in the head. The eyes are forward-facing and move relatively little to track side-to-side movement; scanning up and down takes a lot more effort.

Young babies find reflective surfaces such as mirrors quite interesting. Your baby's developing social awareness helps him begin to acknowledge "the baby in the mirror," but he probably won't be able to identify the image as himself until his second year. ("That baby's always there. Who is he?")

Sometime between 3 and 8 weeks, your baby may develop some head control when being lifted from the crib in a face-up position. These skills are part of the development of balance and posture.

Sometime between weeks 6 and 12, baby's peripheral vision from side to side improved from a quarter of a circle (90 degrees) to a full half circle (180 degrees).

You've probably noticed that your baby's social smile appears more readily now than before. At first it took smiling, touching or tickling, talking, and/or leaning close to bring it on. Now your baby may begin to smile in response to your smiling and nodding without any additional stimulation. Sweet!

Check This Out Your baby's brain will actually *double* in volume from birth to age six months!

Did You Know? How can you help your baby grow a world-class brain? Easy. Provide optimum amounts of high-quality nutrition, physical affection, rest, freedom from stress, health safeguards, and interesting things to smell, taste, touch, hear, and study.

Having a baby can be a scream.

JOAN RIVERS

56
DAYS OLD

DATE:

notes

P By two months, infants are generally feeding about six to seven times a day and consuming about 4.2 ounces (120 ml) per feeding. Breast-fed babies still self-regulate.

C Circular eye coordination continues to improve. Move a brightly colored object in a "rainbow arch" (180-degree half circle) from one side of the baby to the other. By the time she is between two and three months old, she may be able to follow the object's path for about ten seconds.

S Beginning at about eight to twelve weeks of age, your baby may begin to display some pre-ferential behavior toward the primary caregiver. For example, the baby might cry, smile, and vocalize more to the primary care person than to anyone else. This stage in the process of forming an affectionate bond with caregivers is called attachment-in-the-making.

Week 8 ends

The sun never again shone as in the first days of my existence.

NOEMIA DA SOUSA

57
DAYS OLD

DATE:

(P) If baby is prescribed medicine, don't mix the medication with breast milk or formula. Your baby might not drink all the liquid, so he therefore might not receive a full dose of medicine.

(C) By about this time (eight weeks of age), babies can remember a reaction to an event when they have not reexperienced it for two weeks, but only under special circumstances. Try this: Infants can learn to move an overhead mobile by kicking one of their legs that is attached to the mobile by a ribbon. If the mobile is set up again within two weeks of their initial experience, baby can usually remember how to make the mobile move by moving her leg.

(S) While all types of sights and sounds can enliven your baby's senses, there is still nothing more fascinating to the human infant than another human's face and voice. Offer your baby plenty of opportunities to gaze at you and hear your voice. You will always be your baby's favorite toy!

Did You Know? Ninety-five percent of newborns measure between 18 and 22 inches (46 and 56 cm) in length. Only 5 percent of the total are shorter or taller than the norm. One word of caution—your baby's length at birth has little relationship to his adult height.

The decision to have a child is both a private and a public decision, for children are our collective future.
SYLVIA ANN HEWLETT

58 DAYS OLD	DATE:

| 59 DAYS OLD | DATE: |

P At about this time, your baby begins to produce his own antibodies as the immune
protection he received prenatally begins to decline.
The inoculation program exists to provide a level
of protection that baby's weak immune system
can't supply.

C Between one and three months of age, your
baby may be startled by sounds that she
perceives as sudden or loud. When startled, your
baby may stiffen, blink, contort her eyes, extend
her limbs, fan out her fingers and toes, and/or
cry out.

S By two months of age, babies are much more
interested in faces than objects or features.
The little social animal is awakening.

P Your baby may gain ½ pound (8 ounces or
225 g) by the end of this week. That weight
gain is fairly typical and considered healthy during
this time in your baby's life.

C From two months of age on, your baby's memory for a learned association—remembering a
one-time event and her reaction to it— may improve
rapidly. For example, your baby may display some
wariness if she was left to cry in another baby's crib
and is now placed in that crib again.

S Learned associations can also be made to
events with auditory or tactile cues. For
example, if you greet your baby when you walk
into her room (auditory), she may expect you to
pick her up. In addition, if you place your hands
around baby's trunk and under her neck (tactile),
she may expect you to lift her to your shoulder.

Did You Know? Because their nervous system is so new,
babies may actually have a delayed response of three or
more seconds after a startling event.

Kath: Can he be present at the birth of his child?
Ed: It's all any reasonable child can expect if the dad was present at the conception.

JOE ORTON

60 DAYS OLD	DATE:

61 DAYS OLD	DATE:

Ⓟ Arm and leg thrusts during play become particularly pronounced and vigorous by about this time (two months). Your baby's muscles are getting stronger and more effective in moving his limbs. (If we could harness all this clean energy, babies could light up whole cities!)

Ⓒ Now that your baby has had some practice looking at people, by about three months of age, she may begin to show some interest in looking at objects.

Ⓢ The growth rate is so rapid now that your baby literally grows right before your eyes. The increase in length during this first year is concentrated mainly in the trunk, so baby's torso will look long in relation to his limbs, and he's still got a big head.

notes

Ⓟ Tactile stimulation—in the form of comfortable physical contact—is thought to play a key role in the development of trust. Make sure your baby gets plenty of hands-on contact and comforting.

Ⓒ At two months of age, infants like yours seem to spend more time looking at vertical lines—open doors, the spines of books, and so on—than horizontal ones (which caught their attention first).

Ⓢ The more positive or productive the infant-caregiver interactions are, the more closely attached each usually feels toward the other.

Did You Know? Babies spend a long time studying new faces and more time smiling and responding to familiar ones. This difference is thought to indicate a memory for familiar objects and people. Thus, besides the pleasure of their company, another reason why babies tend to prefer their primary caregiver is that he or she is simply more familiar.

Check This Out Play this game with your baby: Sit her on your lap at a table and place a 1-inch (2.5-cm) cube on the table before her. Does she look at the table? Does she look at the cube?

It takes three to make a child.

E. E. CUMMINGS

62 DAYS OLD	DATE:

63 DAYS OLD	DATE:

Ⓟ Mouthing helps infants explore the properties of objects—texture, temperature, taste, and so on. The mouth is full of nerve endings, so baby gets lots of information this way. If your baby has a hold of your finger or clothing, you might get mouthed, too!

Ⓒ Now that your baby has had some practice listening to people, he may begin to show an interest in the sounds objects make and be able to identify them by looking.

Ⓢ Young infants interact socially by crying, vocalizing, sucking, clinging, reaching for, and molding their bodies to those holding them front-to-front. People usually interpret these behaviors as signs that the baby "wants" or "likes" them.

Ⓟ Your baby doesn't need any other liquid but milk. Formula sustains, but breast milk is a self-contained superfood. Babies get all the water they need in the milk they drink.

Ⓒ By about this time (two or three months of age), because your baby's hands are open more often than closed, she may be able to grasp a rattle or similar object briefly on her own.

Ⓢ Sometime between two and four months of age, your baby may begin to study his own hands. This behavior is called *hand regard* and marks one of the first steps in the development of self-awareness.

Did You Know? Good news! Your baby's crying has probably reached its peak. Crying should taper off between now and the end of this month (Week 13).

Check This Out Play this game when your baby is lying in her crib: Hold a bell and a rattle about 8 inches (20 cm) apart above her head. Gently shake one, then the other to make a sound, and alternate slowly between the bell and rattle several times. Your baby's eyes should move back and forth at least three times in response to the sound, particularly by the time she is four or five months old.

Week 9 ends

Keeping house is like threading beads on a string with no knot at the end.
ANONYMOUS

64 DAYS OLD	DATE:

65 DAYS OLD	DATE:

(P) Sometime between one and two and a half months, your baby may begin to do more than merely grasp an object in his hand. He may wave it about, examine it, tilt it back and forth, or use both hands to finger it.

(C) Locating the source of a sound is an important skill that connects babies to their world by letting them know what they're dealing with and where it is.

(S) After birth, your baby's individuality—her temperament or personality—is expressed as her unique style or manner of behaving. You know a little bit about the kind of person your baby is already.

(P) Two or three weeks ago your baby could probably hold his head at a 45 degree angle while lying on his stomach. The next feat of heavy lifting increases the angle to 90 degrees. He should be able to hold the position for several seconds before slowly lowering his head. Expect that accomplishment sometime during months 3 and 4.

(C) Sometime between weeks 8 and 15, your baby may have the eye-hand coordination to begin to carry an object from her hand to her mouth.

(S) By about this time (two to three months of age), your baby will start to make sounds resembling squeals, laughter, and chuckles. (You will love this!) Squealing is usually well established by five months of age.

I watched you with that baby—that other woman's baby. You looked—well, nice.

JOHN WAYNE

Did You Know? Where does temperament or personality come from? Babies are born with genetic predispositions toward certain behaviors. Behaviors that are strongly predisposed are more likely to be expressed than those with weak predispositions, but the baby's family, culture, circle of friends, et cetera can also influence outcomes. Developmentally, it's always nature *and* nurture.

Check This Out Play this game with your baby: Let him hold a red ring or any other graspable object in his hand during free play. What does he do with it?

66 DAYS OLD   DATE:

P When grasping was automatic, parents had to pry open baby's fingers to release the object. (Where are the Jaws of Life when you need them?) By about this time (two or three months of age), your baby may be able to grasp a rattle or similar object briefly, then let go of it on her own.

C By the end of the third month, your baby's ability to see accurately may be twice as good as it was at birth.

S *Rhythmicity* is a temperament characteristic that ranges from high (predictable) to low (unpredictable). At about two months of age, predictable babies have regular feeding and sleep habits; unpredictable babies feed and wake at different times each day.

67 DAYS OLD   DATE:

P Babies are "stomach breathers," moving their abdomen rather than their chest when they breathe. That type of movement is natural and generally not associated with panting or breathlessness.

C Beginning around two months of age, your baby probably started to manipulate objects—like a brightly colored ring or rattle—in a simple way when he held them. Advanced manual manipulation is a skill that will usually develop by four months of age.

S Infants between two and four months of age can be trained to increase vocalizations, sucking, smiling, and head-turning in response to parents' smiles, pats, and praise (among other things). Notice these reactions in yourself and the behaviors they encourage.

IMPORTANT Because their system is so immature, infants are more prone to dehydration than older children.

Did You Know? Your positive attention and physical contact are powerful rewards. Also, keep in mind that inattention and physical distance are powerful punishers that can discourage desirable actions and activities.

Children always want to look behind mirrors.

JOSEPH JOUBERT

| 68 DAYS OLD | DATE: | 69 DAYS OLD | DATE: |

P As early as last week, your baby may have developed the grip strength to retain definite hold of a finger or object placed in his hand. Baby's ability to grip securely and on purpose is usually established by the end of the third month.

C In this week, your baby can probably move her gaze from one object to another.

S Mood quality is a temperament or personality characteristic that ranges from positive to negative. At about two months of age, babies with positive moods are generally smiling and happy; negative babies tend to fuss or cry frequently.

notes

P Sometime between eight and fifteen weeks, your baby may begin to grasp an object briefly between the fingers and the palm of his hand. This is called the *ulnar-palmar grasp*.

C By this time (Week 10), babies are more interested in looking at a picture of a human face with both eyes and eyebrows than a face with either eyes or eyebrows alone. (Tattooed eyebrows, anyone?)

S Sometime between days 9 and 21, your baby's eyes were probably able to follow the movement of a person who walked back and forth within easy view. This more-or-less automatic tracking will be replaced by more advanced visual tracking by the time baby is three to four months old.

Did You Know? If you can understand your baby's needs and her individual temperament, you can predict how your baby might respond to a particular situation or person. Then you can tailor her experience to minimize distress and promote positive outcomes, and that's easier on everyone!

Check This Out Try this: Place a 1-inch (2.5-cm) cube in each of your baby's hands. What does she do with them?

Biology is the least of what makes someone a mother.
OPRAH WINFREY

70
DAYS OLD

DATE:

notes

P Although movement automatically attracts baby's visual attention, he has to learn how to move his eyes to focus on a stationary object. This skill is usually well established between now and the end of the month.

C Being able to move her eyes and fix her attention on an object is one of your baby's most fundamental visual skills. But it's a different accomplishment from visual tracking. In tracking, the object moves and the eyes follow; with eye readiness, moving the eyes toward an object or from one object to another is voluntary, not automatic.

S What does your baby seem to like or dislike? Start to catalog this information, because the better you understand your baby, the more smoothly things can go for everyone.

Week 10 ends

Talk to the child, of things which he knows, connected in a pattern of his own experience, in terms with which he is familiar.

MARY STEICHEN CALDERONE

71 DAYS OLD	DATE:

72 DAYS OLD	DATE:

℗ This is another month when your baby is expected to grow about 1 inch (2.5 cm) in length.

© Your baby is getting better at judging the distance of objects from his eyes and closing them for protection. He may blink when you move your hand or a toy toward his face.

§ Prompt, positive interactions with baby that form an affectionate bond predict baby's secure attachment to the primary caregiver. And since the quality of the infant-parent attachment influences all of the baby's future interactions, promoting bonding through synchrony is a top priority!

Did You Know? The comfort that the securely attached baby feels in the parent's presence doesn't just "happen." It develops with effort, patience, and practice from everyone involved.

Love Notes Even though your baby is young, she needs your praise and approval. If you seem pleased with what baby does or says and convey that feeling physically and/or verbally, she will be more likely to be pleased with herself, and the bond between the two of you can deepen.

℗ By the end of this month, the areas of your baby's brain that receive input from the senses and those that control the movement of her hands, arms, and upper trunk are relatively mature. That means that your baby's ability to move from place to place may enable him to use his senses to explore his world.

© Sometime between 5 and 8 weeks, your baby began to turn her eyes toward an object (like a ring) held 30 degrees or so past her midline. Holding or fixing that gaze is a task that begins now.

§ Adaptability is a temperament characteristic that ranges from "adjusts easily to new events" to "adjusts with difficulty." At about two months of age, babies who adjust with difficulty are startled and distressed by sudden noises and resist diapering; infants who are easy enjoy bath time.

Parental love's the only real charity going.

ABBIE HOFFMAN

notes

DATE:

74
DAYS OLD   DATE:

P A baby around two to three months of age tends to hold his head predominantly erect when sitting rather than letting it fall forward.

C Sometime between two and six weeks of age, your baby probably began to turn her head freely to visually explore her environment when brought into a room. Voluntary visual inspection of her surroundings is usually well established by the end of this month.

S By the end of this month, your baby has studied faces long enough to be able to identify his primary caregiver and to distinguish between some facial expressions of emotion, like happy and angry.

73
DAYS OLD   DATE:

P By about this time (two to three months of age), your baby —whether on his stomach or his back—will tend to have his head aligned with his backbone rather than turned to one side.

C The first evidence of a developing attention span is your baby's ability to hold her gaze on an object or person and "study" it.

S By about three months of age, behavior exchanges between you and your baby can mimic conversation. Most often, adults say or do something to the baby, wait for a response, and then say or do something again. Right now conversation is more about taking turns than sending messages, but it's just as sweet.

Did You Know? In order to get the oxygen their bodies need, babies have to breathe twice as fast as their parents!

Wisdom leads us back to childhood.
BLAISE PASCAL

75 DAYS OLD	DATE:

76 DAYS OLD	DATE:

By this time (here's hoping), your baby can be soothed more readily and seems more settled into his daily rhythm.

Babies the age of yours are energized by interesting experiences. They may move more and vocalize more, and their faces become more animated when they are doing something that they enjoy. It's wonderful to see a baby light up! (Now that's sustainable energy!)

What if your baby is difficult? What if your baby is negative? Does that mean her traits are less advanced or that her characteristics aren't as good as other babies? *Absolutely not.* That's just who she is and how she's inclined to approach life. Don't be disappointed. No need to apologize—just explain and accept the way your child is.

IMPORTANT The fact that by a mere three months of age, our babies are already prepared to read emotions on our faces should give us pause.

Check This Out Caregivers should try to avoid exposing baby to too much, too often. A baby who is overstimulated may feel overwhelmed instead of overjoyed. Take your cue from the baby—if she seems overwhelmed when entering a busy environment or presented with several new objects, try to introduce her slowly to single elements in the room or show her just one object at a time.

It's typical for a baby of about three months old to sag at the knees when held standing with his feet on a hard surface (great-grandmas do, too).

A baby of almost three months can pay attention to a sound or focus on a visual image for three or more seconds, especially if she is interested in it.

The quality of the infant-parent attachment influences all the baby's future interpersonal interactions. Outside of subsistence needs, *nothing* is more important than bonding and making an emotional connection with your child.

A multitude of small delights constitute happiness.
CHARLES BAUDELAIRE

77 DAYS OLD

DATE:

notes

P By the end of this month, your baby may be able to hold on to a large plastic ring without dropping it right away.

C By now, your baby should be pretty good at making small throaty sounds, vowel- and consonantlike sounds, and grunts, coos, sighs, gurgles, explosive squeals, and blowing bubbles, just to name a few.

S Fathers who fed and diapered their babies in the hospital or birthing center tend to do more caretaking at home. Such is also the case for fathers of babies delivered by cesarean section.

Check This Out What sounds do you hear baby vocalize? Jot them down here:

Did You Know? It's not really the father's presence at the birth that affects later interactive behaviors with the baby or his emotional bond to him; it's the father's attitude toward fathering and his relationship to the mother of the baby that does.

Week 11 ends

A man never stands as tall as when he kneels to help a child.

KNIGHTS OF PYTHAGORAS

78 DAYS OLD	DATE:

| 79 DAYS OLD | DATE: |

By this time, the doll's-eye reflex (head moves, eyes follow) has usually disappeared, and the baby's eyes follow the rotation of his head. This development makes visual tracking easier.

In addition to visual memories of faces and objects, auditory memories of sounds and voices, tactile memories about how things feel, and gustatory (cool word, huh?) memories about tastes, your baby is also cataloging memories of new and familiar scents.

By this time (around three months of age) the mother's voice is more effective in quieting her baby than background noise (the whir of a fan or the sound of a vacuum cleaner). Over the next four weeks, distracting the baby with something to look at works to soothe about half the time.

The buildup of crying that parents may have noticed during the first four to six weeks has probably subsided by now—Week 12. (That's one thing you won't miss!)

By about three months of age, baby can begin to fix her eyes directly on another person's face and make eye contact when that person is talking to her rather than at random. This development marks the beginning of voluntary social interaction.

By this time, your baby can begin to reciprocate positive emotions. For example, your baby may show interest through looking and listening, or signs of pleasure when you smile or laugh.

Did You Know? By this time, your baby probably can be soothed more readily and is beginning to settle into her daily "routine" a little better.

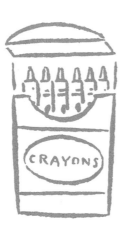

The mark of a good parent is that he can have fun while being one.
MARCELENE COX

8 0 DAYS OLD	DATE:

P Head-holding in a vertical position is usually well established by the end of this month (month 3).

C By about this time (three months of age), baby may lick or smack his lips in response to the sound of feeding preparations. This is evidence that baby is learning to associate the sounds related to feeding with the anticipation of being fed.

S By this month, babies smile broadly at familiar people and stare more soberly at people they don't recognize. This selectivity continues to develop and change during infancy.

notes

_____
_____
_____
_____
_____
_____
_____
_____
_____
_____
_____
_____
_____
_____
_____

8 1 DAYS OLD	DATE:

P The next accomplishment will be for baby to keep her head balanced and in the same plane as her body. That should occur by 4 months.

C Babies nearly three months old can discriminate colors and seem to prefer red and yellow. (Go Arizona State? Go USC? Go Washington Redskins?) Adults prefer blue and green.

S By the end of the first three months, three behaviors have become powerful ways for baby to attract attention and sustain interactions: staring, smiling, and vocalizing.

Check This Out Need to soothe a crying baby? Your presence when you enter the room may help. Infants can usually recover from distress within twenty minutes if they are held and rocked. Remember that holding and rocking doesn't soothe a colicky baby; and food is what a hungry baby needs.

Earthly paradise: the parents young, the children small.
VICTOR HUGO

8 2	DATE:
DAYS OLD	

8 3	DATE:
DAYS OLD	

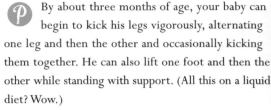

P By about three months of age, baby usually needs support at the shoulders when being dressed while sitting upright.

C By about three months of age, many of the reflexes your baby was born with are fading. That means more of your baby's actions will be intentional and voluntary rather than automatic.

S Babies the age of yours use facial expressions and intonation to communicate their moods, needs, and feelings. Watch their personality shine through!

P By about three months of age, your baby can begin to kick his legs vigorously, alternating one leg and then the other and occasionally kicking them together. He can also lift one foot and then the other while standing with support. (All this on a liquid diet? Wow.)

C During this third month, babies seem to listen to their own voices. It's not clear that they understand that the sound came from them, but they do seem to hear themselves speak in a self-conscious way.

S By two to four months of age, babies are already attuned to conversational turn-taking and may take turns when pauses are provided by their caretakers. (Next month: text messaging!)

Before I had children I always wondered whether their births would be for me, like the ultimate in my gym class failures. And discovered, instead . . . that I'd finally found my sport.

JOYCE MAYNARD

84
DAYS OLD

DATE:

P Exercising their legs by kicking is building core stability for movement, as well as coordination, by kicking one leg and then the other and also kicking both legs together.

C By this time, your baby may begin to understand objects according to more than one dimension. For example, she can begin to associate the way something looks with the way it sounds, feels, and moves. A toy has a characteristic color, shape, sound, and movement.

S Most babies seem to love comforting contact. They relax and smile when being held, rocked, or swung. (Parents do, too.)

Week 12 ends

Presence is more than just being there.
MALCOLM S. FORBES

| 85 DAYS OLD | DATE: |
| 86 DAYS OLD | DATE: |

(P) By three months of age, formula-fed infants drink about 5.5 ounces (165 ml) per feeding and may be feeding five to six times a day.

(C) The same multimodal approach baby takes to understand objects can also be applied to people. For example, baby might recognize mother and other familiar caregivers by a combination of visual, auditory, tactile, and smell-related cues.

(S) By about three months, infants show considerable interest in their environment— excitement when given a toy, reluctance to be left alone, recognition of a parent, and demonstrations of pleasure by bursts of sound and movement.

Check This Out When you move baby's arms and legs, he may respond by relaxing, smiling, vocalizing, or looking at you or his own limbs. (Provided he's not mad or asleep.)

(P) Your baby's digestive tract can now produce saliva, and drooling becomes more common by this third month as saliva output overwhelms the baby's poorly coordinated swallowing reflex. (Yup, it's time for a bib.)

(C) By about this time, your baby's ability to use her eyes in unison to focus on a toy that is moved toward her face (convergence) is usually well developed. Because her eyes turn in to focus on close objects, they may cross temporarily. (Unless that's a family trait, then it's permanent. . . . little joke.)

(S) When baby is fussy, he can be soothed by the sound of a human voice. But as he becomes more familiar with his surroundings, your baby becomes more selective about who he'll respond to.

Aa Bb Cc Dd Ee Ff

I actually remember feeling delight at two o'clock in the morning when the baby woke for his feed, because I so longed to have another look at him.

MARGARET DRABBLE

87 DAYS OLD	DATE:

Ⓟ A refinement of large-muscle (gross motor) skills allows your baby to wave her arms more smoothly, evenly, and symmetrically.

Ⓒ By about three months of age, your baby may pay attention to the sounds of objects as well as people. Ring a bell or shake a rattle behind him about 6 to 12 inches (15 to 30 cm) from his ear. He may quiet for a few seconds after hearing them.

Ⓢ At age three months, the voice that baby is most familiar with is probably her primary caregiver's. At two months, your baby would need the sound *and* touch of the primary caregiver to quiet her down; now she may quiet to just the sound of the caregiver's voice.

88 DAYS OLD	DATE:

Ⓟ Stronger muscles also produce only a slight head lag when baby is pulled from his back to a sitting position.

Ⓒ By this third month, your baby can watch objects travel to the external boundaries of her visual field—a full 180 degrees.

Ⓢ Your baby probably cries when he is uncomfortable or annoyed, and he may vocalize when spoken to or pleased. Baby's emotional range is becoming broader and more varied.

89 DAYS OLD	DATE:

Ⓟ By this time (around three months of age) your baby can probably raise her head and shoulders from a prone position and bear the weight from her upper body and head on her forearms. This is just raw strength—no juice for this baby.

Ⓒ When your baby was a newborn, his eyes seemed to wander. Now he can move his eyes toward a toy or other object and hold his gaze there much more deliberately.

Ⓢ You may be impressed with the effort your baby makes to "talk" when she has your attention and when you speak to her. These conversations benefit baby emotionally because she shares your time and loving attention.

IMPORTANT Your baby has achieved a milestone in visual perception now that he can use his entire visual field to identify and track objects.

notes

_____

The only thing worth stealing is a kiss from a sleeping child.
JOE HOULDSWORTH

90 DAYS OLD	DATE:

(P) Feeding baby solid foods is discouraged until he is four to six months old because his digestive system can't process solids properly until then.

(C) Once again, you can expect your baby's head circumference to increase by about ½ inch (1.27 cm). As the brain cells develop and knit themselves together, they form the foundation for more complex thoughts, feelings, and behavior.

(S) By three to four months, visual stimulation—presenting baby with a toy, for example—becomes increasingly effective in soothing by distraction.

91 DAYS OLD	DATE:

(P) As grip strength improves, babies the age of yours (about three months) can usually clasp and unclasp their hands in finger play.

(C) Your baby should be able to see you from across the room and reach for or bat at objects suspended above her.

(S) Facial recognition has improved. Now (by three to four months of age) your baby can quickly and easily recognize specific faces.

IMPORTANT If you have any concerns about how well your baby sees, check with your health-care provider.

Week 13 ends

If evolution really works, how come mothers only have two hands?

ED DUSSAULT

Week 14 Begins

P By about this time, half of all babies sleep more than fifteen hours and half sleep less.

C If your baby can hold his head up well but can't quite sit on his own, propping him up in a seated position can put him in touch with more interesting sights and sounds.

S Now that it's easier for your baby to recognize familiar faces, she may also begin to reach for the faces she recognizes.

P Your baby's total sleep time may be influenced by her activity level, with active babies typically sleeping less than placid ones.

C From three months of age on, the ways in which infants manipulate and explore objects are increasingly related to the physical properties of those objects. When infants the age of your baby are given a large ball with a rough surface and a small soft object with a lumpy surface, they tend to scratch the ball, which makes an interesting sound; they don't usually scratch the soft toy. Apparently, they expect a rough surface to make a sound, but not a soft one. (An impressive deduction for such a young one!)

S Sometime between three and four and a half months, pleasure may be expressed vocally during free play, toy play, and social interaction.

Did You Know? So has your baby been paying attention? No doubt. Now an object isn't just its name—like a rattle—but is becoming the sum of its properties—hard or soft, rough or smooth, noisy or not, and so on.

Children suck the mother when they are young and the father when they are old.

ENGLISH PROVERB

94 DAYS OLD	DATE:

(P) This is a month of substantial physical growth. Your baby may grow 1 inch (2.5 cm) in height and gain a full 1½ pounds (680 g). (If you have the impression that he's growing out of everything, you're right!)

(C) Your baby continues to coo, gurgle, and laugh out loud. (You must teach that we laugh *with* people, not *at* them.)

(S) By about this time (between three and four months of age), most infants are sleeping more during the night—usually nine to eleven hours—than during the day. (Ah, sweet sleep!)

95 DAYS OLD	DATE:

(P) While your baby is probably able to turn from his side to his back, he may not be able to completely roll from his stomach to his back for at least another month or two.

(C) Your baby may begin to show anticipatory excitement when she expects an adult to lift her, feed her, interact with her, or present a toy. Learned anticipation becomes more common in a few weeks' time—by about four months of age.

(S) Between three and four and a half months of age, baby can express displeasure vocally when play is interrupted, toys are removed, or when he is restrained. (Yikes! That's one mad baby!)

Did You Know? How many times do babies fall asleep each day? Sleep time has been consolidated into long and short naps plus nighttime sleep. Half of all babies are sleeping more than six times a day and half are sleeping less.

Check This Out Your baby might express positive anticipation by increased arm and leg activity, rapid breathing, vocalizing, squealing, or a brightening facial expression. (Of course, it might also be gas.)

Without children there is no real love.

ITALIAN PROVERB

96
DAYS OLD

DATE:

97
DAYS OLD

DATE:

(P) In addition to bearing weight on her arms, your baby can also begin to bear some weight on her legs when held in a standing position.

(C) Listen carefully—your baby may begin to add the consonants *n*, *k*, *g*, *p*, and *b* when he vocalizes. (It won't be long before he can buy a vowel.)

(S) Sometime between three and four and a half months of age, your baby's vocalizations may begin to express satisfaction when she is pleased and eagerness in anticipation of pleasure.

notes

_____

_____

_____

_____

_____

_____

_____

_____

_____

_____

_____

_____

_____

_____

_____

_____

_____

(P) If it hasn't already disappeared, the tongue-thrusting (*extrusion*) reflex is fading. This reflex interferes with spoon-feeding by pushing the spoon out of baby's mouth. (Especially if it's full of that green stuff.)

(C) Sometime between now and five months of age, your baby may begin to voluntarily move his head to follow a dangling ring or toy. This is an improvement over reflex tracking and the doll's-eye reflex because it requires motivation.

(S) Sometime between three and four and a half months of age, you may notice that baby begins to show a distinctive reaction to strangers. The unfamiliar person might receive a questioning look, or baby may stare, frown, withdraw, or cry in the presence of a stranger. This behavior is called *stranger anxiety* and is usually well established by eight months old. The stranger people look to them, the more they'll fret about being in their presence.

Did You Know? Why are babies born with a tongue-thrusting reflex? It seems to help pull milk out of the nipple and allows the baby to push away from the breast or bottle when she's through feeding.

Who judges the world will be its children. It takes a child's mind to judge the world.

GEORGES BERNANOS

98
DAYS OLD

DATE:

Ⓟ Just as in older children and adults, your baby's blood pressure increases and decreases in response to varying types of activity and emotional states.

Ⓒ Your baby's ability to judge distance and to blink if a moving object comes too close should be well established by the end of this month (Week 18).

Ⓢ Between four and six months, your baby may begin to look at his own image in the mirror. (Get behind baby so your image is reflected, too. What's baby's reaction, if any?)

Week 14 ends

A sick child is always the mother's property, her own feelings generally make it so.

JANE AUSTEN

99 DAYS OLD	DATE:	100 DAYS OLD	DATE:

P By the end of this month, your baby may begin to splash in the tub while bathing. Splashing and water play develop strength, eye-hand coordination, shoulder control, and interest in his environment. (Rain gear is advised.)

C Even though your baby has a larger repertoire of vocalizations, crying is still the most common.

S Most babies will suck their fingers or thumbs at some time during infancy. Sucking is a typical response when infants are mouthing objects; sucking also seems to quiet and relax them.

IMPORTANT Pay attention to the sounds that your baby seems to hear, especially if she seems to hear some sounds but not others.

Did You Know? The need for nonnutritive sucking will wax and wane during infancy. Because it usually fades as the child grows older, parents are not contributing to the development of a habit by allowing sucking.

P Between three and four months of age, your baby can probably sit for ten seconds or so when her lower back is slightly supported.

C By the end of this month, your baby may begin to move his eyes toward the rattle in his hand. This action requires the perception that there is something in his hand and that that object is worth viewing.

S You may notice your baby becoming much more interested in *frolic play*. Hold her high above you and move her gently while smiling and talking to her; or hold her in your arms and swing her carefully and playfully to another person. See if she laughs or seems to be having fun.

One of the luckiest things that can happen to you in life is, I think, to have a happy childhood.
AGATHA CHRISTIE

101
DAYS OLD
DATE:

102
DAYS OLD
DATE:

During the first year, weight differences between girls and boys are slight. After the first year, girls tend to lose fat more rapidly than boys. But after age six, girls mature faster, so they increase their weight relative to boys.

Visual acuity has been improving steadily. Your baby can now focus clearly on a ½-inch (1.27-cm) cube held 10 to 12 inches (25 to 30 cm) from his eyes. (It helps him if you can hold the cube still.)

The comfort that the secure baby feels in the parent's presence doesn't just "happen"— it develops with effort and practice.

IMPORTANT Make sure you have baby's car seat properly situated, especially if you take it in and out of your vehicle. Your local law enforcement office or fire station can answer any questions and help you reinstall it.

Don't underestimate your baby's ability to be somewhere other than where you sat her. To prevent serious injury, always use the safety straps on any high chair, stroller, baby seat, or carrier.

In baby's first year, crying is the only language she knows.

Baby's voluntary smile—the social smile—is well established and may be a response to soft talking, smiling, touching, and nodding.

Each child has one extra line to your heart, which no other child can replace.
MARGUERITE KELLY AND ELIA PARSONS

103 DAYS OLD	DATE:

104 DAYS OLD	DATE:

Here's an exercise for directed looking, reaching, and grasping: Seat baby on your lap near a table where a 1-inch (2.5-cm) cube is placed. Does she look and reach? Does she grasp the cube with one or both hands? Place another cube on the table. If baby doesn't pick up one or both cubes, place one cube in each of her hands. See if she can retain them for three or more seconds.

Even though crying is still the most frequent vocalization, it is much less common now than it was during the first three months.

Your baby may begin to play while sitting propped up.

Your baby is probably beginning to roll over and reach for objects. Soon he may begin to bring a toy to his mouth.

While we know that vocalizing occurs spontaneously (even in babies who are hard of hearing), it sometimes looks like babies are also having fun. ("Hey, somebody's got to be the life of the party around here!")

Set aside time each day to give baby your undivided attention. Then look, smile, speak, touch, listen, and snuggle a lot.

notes

_____
_____
_____
_____
_____
_____
_____
_____
_____
_____
_____
_____
_____
_____

When we are young our parents run our life; when we get older, our children do.
VICKI BAUM

notes

105
DAYS OLD

DATE:

℗ You may notice your baby turning and looking at objects when she holds them. Manual manipulation is a skill that is usually well developed by the end of this fourth month.

ⓒ Now that baby is actively picking up and mouthing objects, you'll want to rid your house and garden of flowers, trees, and shrubs that are poisonous to infants and children, and keep items that baby can choke on out of reach.

Ⓢ By four to six months of age, your baby can look and smile at his image in a mirror.

IMPORTANT A baby who can bring an item to his face and put it in his mouth is at risk for accidental suffocation. Keep plastic bags and other chokeable items out of your baby's reach. Make sure parts of larger objects and toys cannot be broken off or become detached.

Week 15 ends

We do not inherit this land from our ancestors; we borrow it from our children.
HAIDA INDIAN SAYING

106 DAYS OLD DATE:

In another week or so your baby should be able to play for a full thirty seconds while sitting propped up. (Whew. Major workout!)

Many common flowers, trees, and shrubs can be poisonous if eaten by infants and children. Check your home and garden for the varieties listed below and remove the risk.

Breast milk from a well-nourished mother, or infant formula, requires no supplementation except for a daily dose of fluoride. Flouride helps build cavity-resistant teeth.

IMPORTANT Poisonous trees and shrubs include: black acacia, black locust, camphor, castor bean, elderberry, euonymus, ivy, jequirity bean, jimson-weed, licorice plant, mock orange, mountain laurel, oak tree, ornamental pepper, potato plant, privet, toyon, and yew. Poisonous flowers include: azalea, carnation, four-o'clock, foxglove, delphinium, California geranium, lantana, lily of the valley, lobelia, lupine, morning glory, nightshade, rosary pea, rhododendron, and vinca.

107 DAYS OLD DATE:

Several reflexes present at birth have disappeared. The disappearance of these reflexes—one effect of rapid brain growth—clears the way for the development of voluntary skills.

Binocular vision—blending the image from each eye into a single picture—is well established.

Having studied her hands and familiarized herself with what her hands can grasp, your baby can now use both hands together to do everything from covering her eyes to pushing away yucky-looking food. Being able to coordinate her hands so that one hand helps the other forms the foundation of all future manipulative skills.

Medical Speak to your health-care provider about fluoride in your baby's diet.

108 DAYS OLD DATE:

By the end of the month, your baby should be strong enough to lift his head or keep it from dropping back while being lowered onto the crib in a face-up position.

By the end of this fourth month, your baby may begin to show a preference for certain toys.

As your baby becomes more interested in spending time with others, she might fuss, protest, or become restless when left alone. (The social animal emerges.)

We cannot tell how much our minds are influenced for life by the fact that we see the world first at a range of two or three feet.

EDWIN MUIR

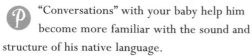

DATE:

109
DAYS OLD

DATE:

110
DAYS OLD

 "Conversations" with your baby help him become more familiar with the sound and structure of his native language.

Reaching, grasping, and retaining skills benefit from practice and involve an interesting mix of large- and small-muscle skills.

Positive and playful interactions between caregiver and infant facilitate baby's development and encourage secure attachment. Have fun with them. They're not little for very long.

IMPORTANT The blossoms of these fruit trees are poisonous if ingested by infants or children: apple, apricot, cherry, peach, and ornamental plum.

Head control is the key to posture and movement and sets the stage for learning and socializing.

Babies will now typically inspect and play with their hands and pull clothing or a blanket over their faces in play. Being able to use both hands to interact with the world is an essential skill that benefits from practice.

It is not possible to spoil your baby by giving him too much love. Indulge your inclination to play, hold, kiss, cuddle, and talk to your baby while he's still a captive audience. Everyone benefits!

Familiarity breeds contempt—and children.

MARK TWAIN

111	DATE:
DAYS OLD	

notes

P While your three- to four-month-old baby can probably play with and shake a rattle in her hand, she usually can't pick it up if dropped. (This changes to "can pick it up but doesn't want to" when she's older.)

C Toward the end of the fourth month, your baby may begin to show a preference for certain toys and may become excited when he sees specific people.

S Even though your baby may smile and vocalize at her image in a mirror, she probably won't realize the image is her own until she's at least fifteen months old.

Check This Out The idea that your baby does something that he takes pleasure in doing is a milestone accomplishment. This action requires self-awareness as well as a remembered evaluation of the experience.

Week 16 ends

Although there are many trial marriages, there is no such thing as a trial child.

GARY WILLS

DATE:

112
DAYS OLD

(P) Even though your three- to four-month-old baby can probably play with and shake a rattle placed in his hand, he probably can't pick it up if dropped.

(C) By about this time (four months of age), your baby should be able to laugh out loud (Okay, baby. Why did the chicken cross the road?) and show interest in new or unusual objects.

(S) Caregivers should try to avoid overstimulating the baby with an onslaught of toys, TV, and play-dates. If she is bombarded with too much too soon, she may feel overwhelmed instead of overjoyed.

DATE:

113
DAYS OLD

(P) Sometime within the next five weeks or so, your baby may be able to hang on to your thumbs while you pull her to a sitting position.

(C) Babies' vocalizations not only reflect language practice but also express emotions. Like yours, her vocalizations tend to change according to her mood and vice versa.

(S) During play, if the caregiver stops interacting and is silent or motionless for thirty to sixty seconds, the baby may show signs of confusion, displeasure, or sadness.

IMPORTANT Overstimulation is especially problematic for premature infants, who are easily overwhelmed and require a lot more time to get used to even low-intensity activities than full-term babies.

DATE:

114
DAYS OLD

(P) By this time (about four months of age), your baby may be able to roll from one side to the other, or from her back to her side.

(C) One of baby's first cognitive tasks is to distinguish the food source from those things that don't provide food or aren't good to eat. (Later . . . how to tell the difference between restaurants and houses.)

(S) Your baby might watch you demonstrate how to scribble, but he won't necessarily even hold the crayon for several weeks. Baby's fine motor skills still leave a lot to be desired.

Perhaps a child, like a cat, is so much inside of himself that he doesn't see himself in the mirror.
ANAIS NIN

notes

DATE:

115
DAYS OLD

DATE:

P Sometime between three and five months of age, your baby may begin to rotate his wrists freely when manipulating toys. (Apparently, it takes a while for baby's brain to figure out how to move those joints!)

C By this time (about four months of age), your baby is beginning to learn what her fingers can do and may practice directing them during finger play.

S If the caregiver is constantly pinching, poking, or tickling, and baby is not in the mood for such play, he might react with frustration, distress, anger, or withdrawal. (He/She who pokes: Beware.)

Did You Know? Babies change position for the same reasons that children and adults do: for pleasure or comfort, curiosity, to relieve boredom, to get closer to something interesting, or just because they can!

A child is not a vase to be filled but a fire to be lit.
RABELAIS

116 DAYS OLD   DATE:

P Sometime between four and five months of age, your baby may begin to show no head lag when pulled to a sitting position. In fact, her head may actually lead her chest in the forward motion to sitting.

C At four months, infants usually develop a reach and grasp that is better coordinated because baby can now explore an object using a combination of his senses. If he can begin to understand whether the object is big or soft or hard, then grasping can be more successful.

S Hold your baby to your chest and bend forward slowly. Babies around four months of age usually enjoy the change of position and the physical contact. Notice your baby's head position— she may begin to balance her head even when her body is tilted.

117 DAYS OLD   DATE:

P Food allergies can be one consequence of introducing solid foods too early.

C When your baby is about four months of age, you may notice that he tends to look back and forth between the object that he's trying to grasp and his hand. This strategy persists until he's about five months of age.

S Sometime between three and six months of age, your baby may begin to show a marked preference for her primary caregiver by looking, smiling, and following the caregiver's movements more than others when there is a choice.

Check This Out At this time, if not before, infants seem to understand that objects are things that have a mass in the three-dimensional world and have visual, tactile, and sometimes auditory properties. Infant-level physics? Move over Einstein!

Kids are the only future the human race has.

WILLIAM SAROYAN

118 DAYS OLD

DATE:

119 DAYS OLD

DATE:

(P) There's no evidence that a baby's diet is nutritionally enhanced when solids are fed to babies younger than four months of age.

(C) During the first four months, infants tend to notice objects directly in their line of vision. They can visually "lock onto" a slowly moving object until it disappears from sight. Once it is out of sight, it is also out of mind, and they tend to show no further interest.

(S) Some parents insist that their baby play with a toy in only one way—a spoon is a utensil for eating, not throwing, for example. Relax and take a lesson from your child. If he wants to put the little bear in his ear, let him (as long as it's safe) and see what he does next. You be the student this time.

notes

(P) For the first four or five months, parents are encouraged to feed baby only milk. Breast is still best.

(C) The "out of sight, out of mind" stage means that infants seem to experience life as though they are watching TV—whatever happens is only happening right there in front of them. Life is unpredictable and varied, and when it goes off, that's it. It's over.

(S) Sometime between three and six months of age, your baby may begin to explore his surroundings. Using his primary caregiver as a safe base, he may venture farther and farther as he becomes more mobile. However, if he becomes uncertain or frightened, he may return to the caregiver to cling or be held.

Week 17 ends

Raising children is like making biscuits: it is as easy to raise a big batch as one, while you have your hands in the dough.

ED HOWE

120 DAYS OLD DATE:

P Right now, your baby may be able to roll from his back to his side because of the *neck-righting reflex*—when baby's head is turned to one side, the body will follow on that side. When that reflex disappears (in about a month), he'll be able to roll on purpose.

C At this time, the hands may rapidly transfer objects from the mouth to a position where eyes can explore them, too. In this way, your baby can compare objects across two sensory systems.

S There is much more interaction during play now than when the baby was under three months of age. Babies at this age tend to show more interest in specific toys and people who might be ready to play. Parents raise their kids up to let them go; and this is when that starts—when they're barely four months old.

121 DAYS OLD DATE:

P Sometime between four and six months of age, your baby may begin to bang her hand, or an object in her hand, in play. Most babies seem to enjoy playing this way (and some grow up to be rock stars and ultimate fighters).

C Infants' look-and-reach approach helps them grab on to everything in sight. Instead of vigorously sucking on every object they hold, sucking changes to mouthing—a more refined way of exploring their world!

S A baby's willingness to be separated from the primary caregiver does not imply rejection or unhappiness. It's simply about expanding their world.

122 DAYS OLD DATE:

P Sometime between three and four months, your baby may be able to sit momentarily without support.

C See what happens: Slowly "walk" a toy in front of baby when he's seated at a table. Then make the toy disappear under a cup. Does his gaze linger on the cup? Does he turn away?

S If you laugh when your baby laughs, you can create a delightful exchange that can volley back and forth several times and build in intensity and fun!

But a child only makes moral progress when he is happy.
The true maxim runs that if we are happy we shall be good.

HOMER LANE

notes

123
DAYS OLD

DATE:

𝓟 Sometime around four and five months of age, your baby may begin to use her thumb for reaching and grasping (the *pincer grasp*), in addition to her fingers and palm.

𝓒 Using both hands together was initially linked to mouthing but now includes holding out an item for visual exploration, too.

𝓢 One of the first intercoordinations between hand and mouth allowed your baby to find his fingers and suck. Babies who suck their fingers or thumbs have a ready means of calming themselves.

Did You Know? Using the thumb independently of the fingers in reaching and grasping is a major milestone in fine motor coordination. (It also helps expose all the stuff in the carpet that defies the vacuum cleaner.)

The only thing children wear out faster than shoes is parents.
JOHN J. PLOMP

124
DAYS OLD

DATE:

125
DAYS OLD

DATE:

P Sometime between four and five months of age, your baby may be able to guide her lips to the rim of a cup.

C Not only can your baby probably fix his gaze on a small object, but he can reach for it as well. (Sometimes those little arms are pretty long!)

S Sometime between four and five months of age, babies become interested in interacting with just about anything close to them that they notice.

P One ironic thing about infants and accidents: Babies should be safest at home, but they're actually much more at risk there. Babies spend the bulk of their day at home, where there may be less supervision than when baby is elsewhere. Be vigilant.

C Around this time, you may notice that your baby is beginning to pay attention to an object that falls and makes a noise.

S If your baby's activity level was more sedate at two months of age—moving little during sleep and other activities—she may tend to be more sedate at four to six months, playing alone quietly with her toys.

Check This Out Play this game with your baby: Seat your baby at a table and hold a metal spoon over the edge of the table on the child's side. Now when he looks at it, let the spoon fall noisily to the floor. Does he seem to hear the sound? Does he turn and look at the floor?

Did You Know? Being able to touch her lip to a cup is a developmental milestone associated with feeding.

In our childhood we know a lot about hands since they live and hover at the level of our stature. . .
VLADIMIR NABOKOV

126
DAYS OLD

DATE:

P Sometime between four and five and a half months of age, your baby may begin to transfer an object deliberately from one hand to another.

C You can stimulate your baby's hearing at this age by exposing him to different types and intensities of sounds. (How about some Mariah, the Stones, and a little country and western?)

S Infants the age of yours seem to enjoy mirror play. Place or hold your baby in front of a mirror so he can study the reflected image. What does he do?

Week 18 ends

Every generation must go further than the last or what's the use of it?
MERIDEL LE SUEUR

Week 19 Begins

127 DAYS OLD	DATE:

128 DAYS OLD	DATE:

(P) Although falls are most common after four months of age, when the infant has learned to roll over, falls can occur at any age. Be watchful.

(C) Dangle a red ring by a string within easy reach of your baby, or hand the ring to her and watch how she manipulates it. Does she look at it? Does she mouth it?

(S) Babies between four and six months old laugh more in response to touch (like tickling) or things that make sounds (like a squeaker).

IMPORTANT Make sure you never place an unattended baby on a raised surface.

(P) By the time your baby is five months old, she may reach more with a single hand than with both hands at once. The hand involved in reaching won't consistently be the right or left but probably will be the hand that's closest to the object.

(C) Now this takes a clever little mind: Sometime between four and five and a half months of age, your baby begins to use one object to retrieve another. (Like when something rolls under your car and you try to reach it by using your shoe or a stick. This is when that strategy gets its start!)

(S) The five-month-old infant and her caregiver interact in a pattern called a *reciprocal exchange*. In exchange for the adult's participation, the baby can offer smiling, laughter, vocalization, and body language.

Self-esteem is as important to our well being as legs are to a table.
LOUISE HART

129
DAYS OLD

DATE:

P Sometime between four and six and a half months, your baby may begin to roll from his back to his stomach. (Yep, crawling is just around the corner.)

C More activity in the reach-and-grasp depart-ment: Now your baby may attempt to reach for and grab just about every item she sees, even though she may not be successful.

S The back-and-forth pattern of the reciprocal exchange sets the foundation for conversation.

Check This Out Rolling from back to front is harder than rolling from front to back. You can offer your baby an incentive to practice by placing a toy at his side but just out of his reach.

130
DAYS OLD

DATE:

P Sometime between six and eight months of age, your baby may begin to pull herself to a sitting position, using a chair or other nearby object for support.

C Your baby may add some new speech sounds to his vocabulary in the next few weeks, so listen carefully.

S Because your baby has new body language and vocalizations to add to any conversation, she can start to contribute a lot more to the exchange. (Even so, when it's her turn, there's still quite a bit of pretending on your part that she understood and responded. It's still great fun!)

God, parents, and teachers can never be sufficiently thanked and repaid.
MARTIN LUTHER

131 DAYS OLD — DATE:

Your baby's eye-hand coordination is developing now. He may want to hold the bottle himself or help guide the spoon.

Allow your baby to lay unclothed on rugs or towels and to move her arms and legs for tactile stimulation.

Your four- to six-month-old will also begin to communicate his moods and emotions through vocal cues and body language. For example, a smile or a laugh may translate into "I like it" or morph into "I'm excited now, but I might be distressed soon."

Check This Out The naked-baby-on-the-furry-rug scene makes a great blackmail photo to use when your baby grows up and starts dating! Don't miss out!

132 DAYS OLD — DATE:

Within the next two weeks or so (by month five), your baby can begin to shift his weight back and forth when on hands and knees in preparation for crawling.

Babies as old as yours (four to five months) can begin to pay attention by looking or listening for thirty seconds or longer. Babies with longer attention spans can learn about the objects and people in their environment and reorient if something changes; babies with shorter attention spans may turn or look away even when there's something fun or interesting in front of them.

During the reciprocal-exchange interaction, watch for the four- to six-month-old infant to avert her gaze. Turning or looking away may be the baby's way of saying "things are getting overwhelming for me."

133 DAYS OLD — DATE:

Your baby is probably getting better and and better at reaching for a toy.

By six months of age, you might notice that your baby adjusts his posture to see an object or person better.

Your baby's overall pattern of eye contact, smiling, and energetic vocalizations may be read as "I love you" or "You make me very happy." An infant who gives love this way can be a very easy baby to love in return. And if the love isn't quite so forthcoming, just keep workin' at it.

Week 19 ends

We can only learn to love by loving.

IRIS MURDOCH

1 34 DAYS OLD DATE:

P After about four months of age, you may notice that your baby actively examines hand-held toys, such as rings or rattles, and plays with them.

C When babies are two months old, they tend to look at their hands. Now at five to six months of age, they spend more time looking at the objects held in their hands.

S The way that your baby smiles, makes eye contact, and vocalizes in the presence of her caregivers suggests that she recognizes them as special people.

1 35 DAYS OLD DATE:

P A typical five-month-old baby will pick up a toy, look at it, feel it, turn it over, shake it, listen to it, and place it in her mouth. (The specific sequence varies, of course.)

C At about five months of age, your baby may continue to look at an object or person who fades out of view.

S The way that infants experience and recover from distress varies widely. Among infants four to six months old, the interval of peak intensity lasts anywhere from two to three minutes to more than thirty minutes. (Who knows whether you've got a Drama Queen or King or a kid who's quick to recover. It's all in the luck of the genetic draw.)

notes

Be gentle to all and stern with yourself.
TERESA OF AVILA

136
DAYS OLD

DATE:

P A major change in your baby's feeding habits is the addition of solid food to her diet. Tooth eruption is usually beginning, too, and facilitates biting and chewing. (Hopefully, biting *food*, not friends or family.)

C Your baby may be just on the cusp of discovering strategies for retrieving out-of-reach toys or objects. For example, baby may learn to pull the string (or other element) that is attached to the object.

S Infants four to six months old may use a variety of self-soothing strategies such as thumb and finger sucking, body and hair rubbing, clutching a favorite object (like a toy or a blanket), and refocusing their visual attention on something new.

What one loves in childhood stays in the heart forever.

MARY JO PUTNEY

137 DAYS OLD   DATE:

138 DAYS OLD   DATE:

Head control is typically well developed by now and allows your baby to sit with support and to turn his head away when he is finished eating.

As baby adds more vowel and consonant sounds to her vocalizations, she begins to collect those sounds and form them into syllables. See if you hear any of these syllable sounds: "goo," "la," "ma," "mu," "ah," "uh," "eh," "aan," "erg," or "da." Or provide entertainment by saying them yourself!

Infants rely on caregivers a lot or a little to help them manage distress. Some infants are easily distracted, some soothe themselves, and some need a lot of lap time—and everything in between.

Did You Know? The type of problem solving required to obtain a toy that can't be reached has a pretty sophisticated foundation. To develop that skill, your baby needs to understand that he is an entity separate from his surroundings and that he can plan and carry out an action in that environment.

Within another week or so (by about five months of age), your baby can probably push her torso up on extended arms. (Ah, Baby Cobra.)

By about five months of age, most babies can tell the difference between two unfamiliar faces and between a photograph of a person on the one hand and a doll on the other. The reasoning seems to be that there are different varieties of unfamiliar people and photographs.

Eye-hand coordination and voluntary grasping will gradually allow your baby to pick up finger foods and feed himself.

139 DAYS OLD   DATE:

By the time your baby is five months old, she can help pull herself to a sitting position.

Your baby also seems to understand that complex patterns in his visual world can be made up of integrated wholes, like large and small circles and light and dark circles, for example. Pretty impressive, huh? Bring on rocket science!

No matter if babies are inconsolable or easily soothed after distress, caretakers become sources of security when they know what their baby needs and they give it to him.

Reality is something you rise above.
LIZA MINNELLI

140
DAYS OLD

DATE:

notes

P Babies about the age of yours (nearly five months old) are usually coordinated enough to bring their hands together. (It's almost patty-cake time!)

C In about another month, your baby can begin to locate sounds made above his head. Watch for baby to turn his head to the side and then look up or down.

S By the fifth month, you may notice that your baby is a lot more animated during social interactions—moving her arms and legs, having a lot to say, shifting her posture, and expressing emotion on her face to reflect whether she's pleased or displeased.

Week 20 ends

Home is where the heart is.
ELBERT HUBBARD

Week 21 Begins

141 DAYS OLD DATE: _____

P If you decide to use a pacifier, make sure it has a safe design.

C Infants the age of yours can make a variety of speech sounds that vary only slightly from each other (like "buh" and "puh"), yet they seem to know the difference!

S Baby may show more interest in inter-acting with the people he feels connected to. Watch for "bigger," more effusive displays of emotional interest and pleasure on baby's behalf when he's paired with a favorite partner.

142 DAYS OLD DATE: _____

P By the time your baby is about five months of age, she can keep reaching for a toy, even if she fails to obtain it.

C Your baby is probably talking about four times as much as he did during his first month. You'll hear him repeat sounds and add variety to them. (Thank goodness for "anytime minutes"!)

S Your baby still loves to be held or rocked by her caregiver and often seems relaxed and secure in the comfort of her parent's arms.

143 DAYS OLD DATE: _____

P One of the hazards of crawling is that your baby can begin to focus on and locate very small objects. Anything put into his mouth has risk potential for choking.

C Babies about the age of yours—five months or so—actively look for and study faces and objects. Baby still seems especially interested in studying her caregiver's face.

S How does baby love thee? You can count the ways! Look for eye contact, spontaneous smiling, cooing (especially open-mouth sounds like "ahh" and "ohh"), and vocalization in response to your facial expressions and greetings. (The open-mouth "kiss" is still some weeks away.)

IMPORTANT As your baby becomes more mobile and curious, baby-proofing and constant supervision are essential.

When one is a child and has no toys, one is well provided for, because then imagination takes over.

SOREN KIERKEGAARD

144 DAYS OLD

DATE:

145 DAYS OLD

DATE:

Ⓟ Mouthing is a prominent activity for most babies the age of yours.

Ⓒ You may notice that your baby is beginning to react with an angry cry and an angry expression when he is frustrated.

Ⓢ Most infants around the age of yours can recover from distress and crying within fifteen minutes, Drama Queens and Kings notwithstanding. (This recovery time is real progress—it's five minutes faster on average than when your baby was around three months old!)

Ⓟ Babies about the age of yours can now roll over. By about seven months of age, baby may be able to roll from his stomach to his back and from his back to his stomach.

Ⓒ Sometime between now and about six months of age, your baby may begin to smile at her own face in the mirror.

Ⓢ Your turn to play Houdini. Lean over your baby so he is looking at your face, then quickly move out of his range of vision for a few seconds. Does baby's facial expression or behavior show that he noticed your disappearance? Now quickly come back into his range of vision. He should be able to acknowledge your presence with a change of facial expression and behavior.

Did You Know? To your baby, appearance and disappearance may occur by what seems like magic right before their eyes. The "magic" goes away when your baby understands that even though an object or person is outside his field of vision, it continues to exist.

It will be gone before you know it. The fingerprints on the wall appear higher and higher. Then suddenly they disappear.

DOROTHY EVSLIN

146 DAYS OLD

DATE:

147 DAYS OLD

DATE:

Sometime between now and about seven months of age, your baby may begin to sit without support.

Mother and father recognition is usually well established by about this time—the fifth month.

At five months of age, babies can participate in interactive games by anticipating the interactive sequence and responding. For example, you may notice your baby tense her muscles and widen her eyes when you begin a game of peek-a-boo. She may also use her body language and facial expressions to indicate that she wants to play again!

notes

_____
_____
_____
_____
_____
_____
_____
_____
_____
_____
_____
_____

The physical structures that give your baby feedback about the position of his head are located in his inner ears (one on each side). Babies are hardwired to lift their heads to an upright position when their bodies are tilted.

With plenty of experience, babies about the age of yours can pair an object with its sound and glance at an object in response to its sound.

Infants recover fastest from distress and crying if the caregiver is someone the baby feels attached to, vocalizes to baby, and makes interesting faces. (Study pantomime!)

Check This Out Play this game with your baby: While baby is lying in her crib, hold a bell and a rattle above her head and about 8 inches (20 cm) apart. Shake the rattle and then ring the bell several times back and forth. Do you see your baby's eyes move in response to each sound?

Week 21 ends

Children command us by their tears . . .
STENDHAL

148 DAYS OLD	DATE:

149 DAYS OLD	DATE:

P Prevent accidental poisoning by placing medicines, vitamins, and toxic substances like cleaning products and garden sprays out of reach or locked away.

C Your baby's ability to coordinate reaching, grasping, and manipulating the objects in his hands should be fairly well established even though his arm and hand movements might be rather uncoordinated.

S Babies the age of yours typically look and smile at their image in the mirror, and yet there's no indication that they know that they are looking at an image of themselves.

P Two important skills—manual manipulation and visual tracking—should be well established by now, the fifth month.

C During his fifth month, your baby may enjoy activity centers and busy boxes; stuffed animals and soft dolls; household items such as unbreakable bowls, measuring cups, and small boxes; and bath toys that allow him to pour and splash. (They have so much fun that they don't want to get out of the tub!)

S By about this time (five months of age), babies generally tolerate rougher play, active tickling, or mild roughhousing—both girls and boys alike.

Aa Bb Cc Dd Ee Ff

If we discovered that we had only five minutes left to say all that we wanted to say, every telephone booth would be occupied by people calling other people to stammer that they loved them.

CHRISTOPHER MORLEY

150 DAYS OLD	DATE:

℗ Protect your child from dogs and other aggressive animals and humans.

© By about this time (five months of age) your baby may show more interest in looking at a picture of a face with eyes, eyebrows, *and* a mouth than at a face that is missing one or more of these three features.

⑤ You already know that your baby is working on imitating the habits of those around her. It's usually hilarious—and somewhat disarming—to see what looks like *her* interpretation of *your* habits and actions!

notes

_____
_____
_____
_____
_____
_____
_____
_____
_____
_____
_____
_____
_____
_____
_____
_____

151 DAYS OLD	DATE:

℗ Your baby will probably gain about 1½ pounds (680 g) in weight this month. (If you garden, then you know that "growing like a weed" is an apt metaphor for infant development.)

© By about this time, most babies can recognize the feeding bottle, if they are bottle-fed.

⑤ Your baby is getting a clearer sense of activities that he likes and dislikes, and he may attempt to repeat the pleasurable ones.

IMPORTANT Check the surface temperature of baby's car seat and belt before placing her in the seat. Do not leave your baby in the car by herself for even a minute.

To lose patience is to lose the battle.
MOHANDAS K. GANDHI

	DATE:
152 DAYS OLD	

	DATE:
153 DAYS OLD	

(P) Between twenty and twenty-two weeks of age, babies can usually reach for an object placed in front of them or to either side. Baby's favorite is usually a two-handed reach at midline.

(C) The acquisition of large- and small-muscle skills allows much more independent movement and helps your baby interact with his world in a way that helps him figure it out.

(S) As baby matures, she may be able to tolerate some frustration and delayed gratification. Still, it's difficult for most five-month-old infants to be patient, even babies who are tolerant by nature.

(P) Most babies the age of yours (five months or so) can hold their heads upright while lying on their stomachs.

(C) Your baby may watch intently while an adult hides an object underneath or behind something (a napkin or small screen, for example), but he may only remove the barrier to retrieve the object if a recognizable part of the object is visible. (This baby refuses to be outwitted by a shell game!)

(S) As part of their developing sense of intention, infants between five and five and a half months old may become unhappy or frustrated if an activity that they want to begin or continue doesn't happen.

IMPORTANT Do not tie toys across the crib or play-pen—baby might get entangled in the string.

Where there's a will, there's a way, and where there's a child, there's a will.

MARCELENE COX

154
DAYS OLD

DATE:

notes

Ⓟ Babies the age of yours (five months or so) tend to voluntarily grasp an object using the flat of their hand and their third and fourth fingers. (Not unlike Spider-Man—Spider-Baby!)

Ⓒ For safety's sake, offer your baby toys that are smooth and rounded, preferably made of unpainted wood or non-toxic plastic (avoid PVC plastic). Check the source of the materials first.

Ⓢ Infants about the age of yours (five to six months) may begin to attract the attention of others by methods beyond crying. As their communication skills develop, they may call out, use body language, gesture, or display some other behavior as a signal. (Beware of the thrown shoe.)

Week 22 ends

It is better to be loved than feared.
SENEGALESE PROVERB

155 DAYS OLD	DATE:

156 DAYS OLD	DATE:

(P) You've probably noticed that your baby may be able to hold a sitting position with only a slight prop (maybe a pillow or your hands on his lower back).

(C) By about this time (five months of age) your baby can usually see the similarity between an unfamiliar person and his or her photograph.

(S) You'll notice that your baby begins to apply certain strategies that she knows are associated with interesting outcomes to new objects. For example, a baby of five or six months would probably know how to pump her arm up and down in order to shake a rattle. Chances are, she would also "shake" other objects (like a car or a cup) to see if they rattle, too.

IMPORTANT Keep a fire extinguisher in your home. Know where it is and how to use it. Test it periodically along with your smoke detectors.

(P) The iron reserves that a full-term newborn received from his mother before birth begin to diminish about this time—the fifth or sixth month.

(C) As your baby explores her environment, the quality and quantity of her actions seem to become evident to her. For example, "more" and "less" shaking produce different outcomes, as do shaking and pulling the same toy.

(S) Sometime between five and six months of age, your baby may begin to tell the difference between one unfamiliar person and another.

notes

All things at first appear difficult.
CHINESE PROVERB

157 DAYS OLD

DATE:

158 DAYS OLD

DATE:

Ⓟ Over the next few weeks or so, watch your baby's back become more straight than curved—that's the final skill involved in sitting alone steadily.

Ⓒ Babies the age of yours—between five and six months old—are usually able to use their memories to recognize patterns they have been shown two days before.

Ⓢ Before about five months of age, babies tend to smile at humans regardless of the person's expression or tone of voice. But sometime between five and seven months of age, your baby becomes sensitive to the expression on the person's face, smiling at a friendly face and crying or pouting if the face is angry or the voice scolds. (In other words, leave your road rage at the door.)

Ⓟ By five months of age, your baby may begin to hold his head steady while being carried in an upright position or when you are holding him and swaying back and forth.

Ⓒ A five-month-old baby can usually modify her own sounds to resemble those of others, imitating both the sound and its pitch.

Ⓢ While your baby has been smiling at faces for months now, he also may smile in the presence of objects and toys. Smiling becomes especially likely when baby seems to be enjoying himself (watching a mobile or playing with a toy) or when he likes something that he did or that somehow felt successful.

A thorn can only be extracted if you know where it is.
RABINDRANATH TAGORE

159 DAYS OLD   DATE:

160 DAYS OLD   DATE:

(P) Strained or pureed vegetables or fruits should be organically grown and offered plain—without added sugar, salt, or chemicals.

(C) Offering baby semisolid food actually helps her form her first words. The muscles baby develops by chewing and swallowing are the same ones used for speech. (Your pitch: "Here, baby. Eat the yucky green stuff on the spoon. It will build your vocabulary!")

(S) Intentionality—having a plan or purpose in mind—is one of the distinguishing characteristics of the four- to eight-month-old baby. Watch your baby play. See if he intentionally repeats actions that produce pleasing outcomes.

(P) The average length of the longest period of sleep for babies nearly six months old is about six hours. That's nearly twice as long as the average at two months! (Ah, sweet sleep.)

(C) Your baby's ability to see clearly and accurately reaches about 20/200 by the time he is six months old. In other words, baby must be placed within 20 inches (51 cm) of an object to see what a person with 20/20 vision can see at a distance of 200 inches (16.7 feet, or 5 m).

(S) Your baby was primed to focus on the human face at birth and then to shift attention from people to objects as she learns to reach and grasp. Right now your baby is working on including both people and objects in her interactions.

I can't help it. I like things clean. Blame it on my mother. I was toilet trained at five months.

NEIL SIMON

notes

161
DAYS OLD

DATE:

The right amount of fat in your baby's diet is necessary for good health. Fat provides fatty acid to help maintain the health of the skin and hair, insulate body organs from damage by high fevers, provide an energy reserve, and coat the cells in the nervous system to ensure efficient functioning.

By about six months of age, your baby can begin to localize sounds made above his head—baby may turn his head to the side, and then look up or down.

When the language dance becomes well synchronized, and baby moves to what she anticipates you to say and you say what you know baby expects, the exchange is a lot of fun and feels like a real accomplishment. (High fives all around? You can try it, but probably a low ten in the middle, because that's where her hands are.)

Week 23 ends

Keep me away from the wisdom which does not cry, the philosophy which does not laugh,
and the greatness which does not bow before children.

KAHLIL GIBRAN

162 DAYS OLD	DATE:

163 DAYS OLD	DATE:

P Baby's body fat also stores and helps his body absorb vitamins A, D, E, and K. But even a child can have high cholesterol, so get used to including only healthy amounts in your baby's diet.

C Babies the age of yours (about six months old) are just starting to understand the concepts of same and different. If your baby is shown a collection of two types of objects, he can select two of a kind between 50 and 80 percent of the time.

S It's unrealistic to assume that any environment is baby-proof. The best outcomes involve constant vigilance by an adult caregiver, an understanding that babies are naturally curious, and knowing that it only takes a second for baby to get in trouble.

P Within the next week or so (by about six months), your baby's brain may weigh 50 percent as much as that of an adult. (Keep building that gray matter!)

C Your baby's language-learning centers are becoming selective, having heard baby's native language for five months. Now, her brain is starting to organize itself around what it hears—infants learn vowel sounds that are in their native language more rapidly than those that are not.

S As you lean over baby with your hands in a position to lift him, you may see your baby tense his body or shoulders and/or adjust his arms in anticipation.

Check This Out Want to get your baby to laugh? Tickle her; cover your face and say, "Boo!"; say, "I'm gonna get you"; or move in tricky ways—roll over, crawl, or spin like top.

Never worry about the size of your Christmas tree. In the eyes of children, they are all thirty feet tall.
LARRY WILDE

164 DAYS OLD   DATE:

165 DAYS OLD   DATE:

(P) Try this: Offer your baby a two-handled sippy cup and see if she can drink from it.

(C) Your baby's visual tracking skills now include being able to follow a moving object and to focus on the object's point of disappearance.

(S) Babies the age of yours love toys that make sounds. Select carefully—what is interesting to their ears may sound like noise to yours!

notes

_____
_____
_____
_____
_____
_____
_____
_____
_____
_____
_____
_____
_____
_____
_____
_____
_____
_____

(P) It's taken your baby just about six months to hold his hands open rather than closed when not grasping an object.

(C) One conclusion about your baby's behavior that is inescapable is that she continues to practice reaching, moving, and grasping despite many times coming up—literally—empty handed. What motivates babies just like yours to keep trying? (They can't know about money or candy yet, can they?)

(S) While your baby might physically prepare himself to be picked up, those behaviors are in addition to the emotional anticipation of being lifted.

Check This Out Try this game with your baby: Stand behind her outside of her field of vision. Hold a brightly colored ball out 8 to 10 inches (20 to 25 cm) above her eyes with your right hand and a piece of paper in your left hand (or vice versa). Attract baby's attention to the ball and move it slowly (1 inch per second) until it passes behind the paper. Hold the ball behind the paper for five seconds. Do her eyes linger at the vanishing point?

Children are not things to be molded, but are people to be unfolded.

JESS LAIR

166
DAYS OLD

DATE:

notes

P Head balancing has come a long way from the early bobblehead days. Now at about six months of age, your baby can keep his head balanced and in a straight line with his body.

C Mouthing is a skill that your baby still relies on to explore the properties of objects: temperature, texture, wet/dry, movement, and hard/soft.

S The development of a secure attachment helps keep babies safe by keeping them close to their caregivers.

Well done is better than well said.

BENJAMIN FRANKLIN

167 DAYS OLD
DATE:

168 DAYS OLD
DATE:

P If breast-feeding must be discontinued before five or six months of age, your baby will probably be weaned to a bottle. Continue to hold your baby as you feed her so she can memorize even more about your face than she already knows, and you can do the same with hers.

C By about five months of age, infants can begin to imitate sounds and simple gestures.

S A secure attachment also allows the parent to provide stimulation through playful interactions, which develop the baby's interpersonal skills.

Did You Know? The ability to imitate others is a milestone accomplishment for your baby. It forms the foundation for learning more-advanced behaviors.

P Baby's first teeth may appear now, but the normal range for the appearance of the first tooth is anywhere between four months and twelve months! There may be some pain when the crown of the tooth breaks through the gum.

C By the second half of their first year, most infants understand simple discipline, such as the meaning of the word "No," or a remark like "Yuck! Put it down."

S Like children and adults, some babies yield readily to efforts to calm them, while others yield with more difficulty. This characteristic—sometimes called *adaptability*—is fairly stable from one year to the next.

Week 24 ends

With love and patience, nothing is impossible.
DAISAKU IKEDA

169 DAYS OLD	DATE:

| 170 DAYS OLD | DATE: |

℗ By about this time—six months of age—head balancing and head-backbone alignment are generally well established.

© At this point in your baby's language acquisition, her vocalizations probably consist of syllable sounds such as "ma," "mu," "da," "di," or "hi."

Ⓢ In addition, babies about six months of age have already formed attitudes about the people and events in their world. Your baby has definite likes and dislikes and may express these sentiments in her behavior. (Behold the roots of social acceptance and prejudice—at six months of age!)

℗ First teeth may appear now, but later teething isn't connected with any health or developmental problems. Some discomfort may be experienced along with drooling, increased finger sucking, and biting on hard objects. Other children are very irritable, have difficulty sleeping, and refuse to eat.

© Sleep helps baby concentrate and learn when she's awake. Half of babies the age of yours (twenty-five to twenty-six weeks of age) are sleeping a little more than fourteen hours a day and half are sleeping less.

Ⓢ By six months of age, infants are very personable. They may play games such as peek-a-boo when their head is covered by a towel, they may signal their desire to be picked up by extending their arms, and they may show displeasure when a toy is removed or their face is washed.

Did You Know? The ability to put consonants and vowels together to form syllables is a milestone accomplishment because syllables are combined to form words.

Children are curious and are risk takers. They have lots of courage. They venture out into a world that is immense and dangerous. A child trusts life and the processes of life.

JOHN BRADSHAW

171 DAYS OLD DATE:

172 DAYS OLD DATE:

For the next six months, you can expect your baby to gain 3 to 5 ounces (85 to 140 g) each week. (You'll want to shop for larger-size clothing. It's hard to keep up with their growth rate!)

As evidence of your baby's increasing attention span, your baby should be able to turn his eyes and focus on an object for more than two seconds. (That's not a lot of time, but attention span builds on itself.)

If baby stopped crying when comforted or rocked at two months of age, she may also quiet at six months when given a toy during diapering or when the caregiver talks or sings.

notes

If breast-feeding must be discontinued before baby is five or six months of age, weaning should be to a bottle because of the baby's continued sucking needs.

Babies the age of yours (around six months old) are becoming increasingly interested in the world around them. For example, they might adjust their posture so they can see better.

If your baby was generally smiling and happy at two months of age, he probably doesn't complain much now that he's six months of age.

Did You Know? Even without teeth, biting and chewing tend to occur by the time baby is six months old. These oral skills represent milestones in the development of mature feeding.

Start every day with a smile and get it over with.
W. C. FIELDS

173 DAYS OLD	DATE:

174 DAYS OLD	DATE:

P When your baby is held in a standing position, her legs can begin to support almost all her weight. Momentary standing might happen in the next couple of months.

C Your baby may begin to anticipate a variety of events based on learned cues. For example, if he thinks he is going to get to see someone he likes, he may begin to show anticipatory excitement upon hearing footsteps.

S If your baby adjusted easily to change at two months and enjoyed bath time, for example, she may continue to adjust fairly well at six months of age, disliking new faces at first, but now accepting them.

P In general, your baby can be expected to grow about ½ inch (1.27 cm) in height each month until his first birthday. That's 3 whole inches (7.6 cm)!

C If she hasn't already, your baby may begin to show evidence of a budding memory. For example, when she drops a toy, she may begin to retrieve it.

S Babies the age of yours (five to six months old) may easily recognize their parents but are beginning to feel uncomfortable around strangers.

The quickest way for a parent to get a child's attention is to sit down and look comfortable.

LANE OLINGHOUSE

175
DAYS OLD

DATE:

P Around six months or so, your baby may be able to hold his own bottle.

C Babies the age of yours may spontaneously vocalize in a variety of settings and situations. For example, she may "talk" to her toys and to her image in the mirror.

S Even if you have a fairly happy baby, infants around six months of age have frequent mood swings. They can go from crying to laughing with little or no provocation, because the emotional centers of the brain are more prominent than the rational centers. (Everyone with kids can relate.)

Week 25 ends

Wonder is the beginning of wisdom.

GREEK PROVERB

176 DAYS OLD

DATE:

177 DAYS OLD

DATE:

P When your baby is startled, by a loud sound, for example, the Moro reflex is activated. The baby propels his arms out perpendicular to his body and then draws them into his chest. Sometimes these movements are made during sleep. The Moro reflex is taken as a sign of a healthy nervous system; it's actual significance is unclear.

C Of all the colors of the visual spectrum, your baby continues to prefer red and yellow. These colors are bright and easily attract baby's attention.

S Sometime between six and eight months of age, your baby may begin to respond to her own name. If she doesn't seem to recognize her name yet, use it frequently when the two of you interact.

P Within the next four weeks or so (by about seven months of age), your baby may begin to make forward progress of 9 inches (23 cm) or more when he crawls, creeps, hitches, pushes, or scoots from place to place.

C Sometime between now and eight months of age, your baby may begin to show some interest in the details of objects.

S Part of the emotional development of the infant is to express pleasure when engaging in certain activities. One of the activities six- to seven-month-old babies seem to enjoy is tearing and crumpling paper and putting paper in their mouths. (Genetically hardwired to recycle? Who knew?)

Ah! What would the world be to us if the children were no more?
We should dread the desert behind us worse than the dark before us.
HENRY WADSWORTH LONGFELLOW

notes

178
DAYS OLD

DATE:

At twenty-six weeks of age, your baby may continue to consolidate her sleep time into longer and longer episodes, requiring slightly less sleep as she continues to grow. For example, half of all babies sleep five times a day and half sleep less.

Young babies tend to focus on one thing then another, one after another, in a series. If a six-month-old is given two objects, for example, he typically holds on to one and drops the other.

Sometime between now and seven and a half months of age, your baby may begin to actively participate in games. Up until now, your baby could indicate her amusement by smiling or laughing. Active participation means, for example, moving her hands to play pat-a-cake when you do.

Check This Out Try this with your baby: Hold a bell in front of your baby and, while he is looking at it, ring it and then hand it to him. Does he look at the bell by turning it over in his hand? Does he finger the clapper?

Never again in your life will you be so important to a human being. And if you don't enjoy that, you're sunk.
BRUNO BETTELHEIM

179
DAYS OLD

DATE:

180
DAYS OLD

DATE:

At first, cup feeding will be supplemental, but by your baby's first birthday or so, she may be able to hold the cup with two hands and swallow four or five times without choking.

Some actions and interactions laid down as memories at six months of age may be recalled two years later (see below).

As infants demonstrate more attachment to one person, they correspondingly exhibit less friendliness to unfamiliar people. Such behaviors as clinging to the parent, crying, and turning away from the stranger are common.

Did You Know? Can early experiences be stored as memories? When two-and-one-half-year-olds were invited back to a unique laboratory setting where they were repeatedly tested two years earlier, they were more likely to interact with the toys they had had in the laboratory at that time. Thus, children can remember actions they took as infants if the context is rich in reminders.

By about this time, the average infant weighs about twice as much as she did at birth— about 16 to 17 pounds (7.26 to 7.71 kg). Your baby's weight will tend to vary around that average. Enter your baby's actual weight here: _____.

Your baby's ability to solve problems should not be underestimated. Install locks and be sure they stay locked. Use knob covers to prevent your baby from opening doors, and secure exterior doors with a chain-lock or deadbolt.

At six to eight months of age, infants may refuse to go to unfamiliar adults. Parents have usually become definite interactive favorites, and infants know how to attract their attention. (They can scream like the family goat just gored them.)

notes

_____

_____

_____

_____

_____

_____

_____

_____

_____

_____

Solitude is a deep need. Complete inner solitude. To be alone with yourself for hours at a time, with nobody else around, is an ultimate goal. To be all alone, the way a child is alone.

RAINER MARIA RILKE

181
DAYS OLD

DATE:

182
DAYS OLD

DATE:

(P) The average baby measures about 25½ inches (65 cm) in length at about six months. Enter baby's actual measurement here: _____.

(C) By about seven months of age, your baby may begin to discover rhythm in games. He might indicate his familiarity with the cadence or pacing of the game by smiling, screaming, or laughing in anticipation of the exciting parts performed by the caregiver.

(S) Babies about the age of yours tend to turn their heads toward familiar voices and recognize familiar people by smiling and becoming more active.

(P) The head circumference of the average six-month-old baby is about 17 inches (43 cm). Enter baby's measurement here: _____.

(C) By the time your baby is seven months of age, she may begin to sit alone steadily while manipulating toys, turning, or engaging in other actions that take her attention away from the sitting process itself. (It's the infant version of being able to walk and chew gum at the same time.)

(S) By the end of his seventh month, your baby can begin to recognize the same person from different viewing angles, such as profile versus full face. He can also begin to identify similar facial expressions on different faces, and he can begin to distinguish between female and male faces.

Week 26 ends

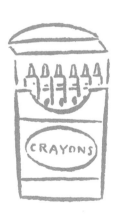

The face of a child can say it all, especially the mouth part of the face.
JACK HANDEY

183 DAYS OLD

DATE:

P Maturation of the respiratory system and increased vocal control help infants produce multiple sounds on a single breath. These sounds usually consist of repeated consonant-vowel combinations like "nananana."

C Beginning about now (six months of age), your baby may repeat two syllables of the same sound during vocal play. While these syllables are not necessarily intended as meaningful, she may be able to repeat two syllables of the same sound on purpose by her first birthday.

S Within a few weeks (by about seven months of age), you may notice that baby is actively seeking close contact with the primary caregiver.

Even when freshly washed and relieved of all obvious confections, children tend to be sticky.

FRAN LEBOWITZ

184 DAYS OLD — DATE:

185 DAYS OLD — DATE:

P An active six- to twelve-month-old is fairly mobile, interested in exploring, and often delighted by big sounds like those the pots and pan lids make in the kitchen. (It can sound like underwater demolition in no time.)

C Sometime between now and eight months of age, your baby may be just beginning to indicate that he recognizes some words as familiar. He might indicate that he recognizes words such as "baby," "up," or "mama" as familiar by changing his facial expression or vocalizing.

S When your seven-month-old baby sees her image in a mirror within easy reach, she should be able to react to the mirror image by moving her head, body, hands, or fingers.

P By about this time (six months of age), your baby's pancreas is probably secreting sufficient quantities of an enzyme that helps extract the nutrients from complex carbohydrates like fruits and vegetables. (The correct question is: What is amylase?)

C Sometime between five and eight months of age, your baby may begin to associate certain outcomes. For example, if baby is given a bell or a rattle and has learned to anticipate a sound or noise from it, he may bring the bell closer to his ear before he shakes it or lean his head down toward the toy.

S By about seven months of age—and about one month after showing attachment to the mother—many babies begin attaching to other members of the family, most often the father or siblings. This affectionate bond is the family's reward for their patience and frequent, positive contact with the baby.

The essential self is innocent, and when it tastes its own innocence knows that it lives forever.
JOHN UPDIKE

| **186** DAYS OLD | DATE: | **187** DAYS OLD | DATE: |

P Around age six months, your baby's ability to use her hands to manipulate objects has increased. She can now hold a bottle, grasp her foot and pull it toward her mouth, and feed herself a cracker. (Time to hit the road with the Baby Traveling Circus.)

C By the time your baby is seven months of age, his vision may have improved enough for him to see objects that are less than 1 inch (2.5 cm) across. His ability to focus on small objects is a milestone achievement in visual perception.

S By the end of this month, your baby may begin to cough or snort to make her presence known. (Ahem! Hellooooww!)

P Despite household items, coins, bits of plastic, and pieces of cloth, food is actually the item most likely to get lodged in your baby's windpipe. The most frequent offenders are hot dogs, candy, nuts, and grapes.

C When your baby is about seven months of age, she should be able to pick one or two cubes from a table or hold a cube in each hand and retain them for three or more seconds.

S In another few weeks—by seven months of age—you may notice your baby imitating actions and noises he has seen and heard around him. (Keep the flatulent members of your family away from your baby at this time.)

I filled out an application that said, "In case of emergency notify. . ." I wrote, "Doctor."
What's my mother going to do?
STEVEN WRIGHT

188
DAYS OLD

DATE:

P In the next month or so, if your baby is held in a standing position, she may begin to bear all her weight on her legs by stiffening and extending them rather than letting her legs and hips go limp.

C Communication during the second six months of the first year seems to involve a conscious intent on the infant's part. That is, babies do not seem to plan for their behaviors to send messages to others.

S Communication does seem to occur, however this is because the people who interact with the baby attribute meaning to her actions. (I'll take that to mean "yes.")

189
DAYS OLD

DATE:

P When your baby starts teething, she may begin to bite to bring relief from teething discomfort. (Try to have something available for her that doesn't have blood vessels in it.)

C Your baby's ability to grasp an object between his fingers and the palm of his hand without including the thumb should be well established by now, six to seven months of age.

S By about this time (about six months of age), baby's self-talk seems to indicate that she likes hearing the sound of her own voice. (Now that's starting out on a positive note!)

Week 27 ends

If your parents never had children, chances are you won't either.
DICK CAVETT

Week 28 Begins

P The world looks entirely different from your baby's vantage point. After you baby-proof your home, get down to your baby's level to see what other things might need attention.

C Your six- to seven-month-old infant may begin to demonstrate taste preferences. For example, he may indicate his dislike of a particular food by keeping his lips pressed closed. (Spitting food out sends a pretty clear message, too, as does feeding it to the dog.)

S Babies about the age of yours (between six and nine months old) are beginning to understand vocal expressions of emotion. They may start to smile in response to a happy voice and frown or become wide-eyed in response to an angry voice.

P If you haven't already done so, introduce your baby to the two-handled sippy cup. Your baby may be able to take one or two swallows from a cup that is held for her.

C Part of learning to communicate is to shadow what others do. For example, you may notice that your baby talks when others are talking. (Has to. Can't get a word in edgewise.)

S Depending on the time of year, evaluate the importance of having baby's picture taken with Santa Claus, the Easter bunny, clowns, or costumed trick-or-treaters. Already sensitive to strangers, baby might find these encounters to be particularly distressing.

notes

Let us furnish [our childrens' lives] reasonably with what is in our power. For that purpose, we should not marry so young that our age comes to be almost confounded with theirs.

MICHEL EYQUEM DE MONTAIGNE

192 DAYS OLD

DATE:

193 DAYS OLD

DATE:

Ⓟ Food allergies occur in about 5 percent of children under three years of age. Introduce foods one at a time and wait four to seven days to note any reactions.

Ⓒ While your baby is learning to read emotion in caregivers' voices, most babies can comprehend facial expressions of emotion (e.g., a smile, a frown, et cetera) by now.

Ⓢ You may notice that your baby seems to understand simple discipline, such as the meaning of the word "no" or a scolding remark like "Get down."

Did You Know? The discomfort your baby is beginning to express when his parent disappears and strangers appear represents a milestone in the development of attachment, memory, and perception.

Ⓟ Finger foods such as teething crackers, raw fruit, or vegetables can probably be introduced by six or seven months. Foods with the lowest allergic potential are carrots, squash, pears, apricots, and peaches.

Ⓒ Your baby's sound-location skills are improving. She now localizes sound by turning her head in a curving arch, just in case the sound source is above her. (Baby radar!)

Ⓢ If, over the last month or so, you have been referring to your baby by name, he may now respond to his name with some indication of recognition.

To a real child anything will serve as a toy.

JOHN COWPER POWYS

194 DAYS OLD	DATE:

P The more calories your baby gets from solid foods, the fewer calories she should be getting from milk. At any age, overfeeding occurs when too many calories above growth needs are eaten.

C By about seven months of age, your baby may begin to transfer objects from one hand to the other to better explore what he's holding.

S Between six and twelve months of age, your baby's social development depends on her interaction with the primary caregivers. Attachment to the parents is increasingly evident during this time and increasingly important.

195 DAYS OLD	DATE:

P When your baby is lying on her back with her face turned upward, you may notice that she spontaneously lifts her head off the surface. This behavior is a milestone

C While your baby will often examine an object by transferring it from one hand to the other, he tends to reach and grasp more often with only one hand than with two.

S One indication of the importance of attachment is that six- to twelve-month-old babies become increasingly alert to their mother's whereabouts and activities.

The bond that links your true family is not one of blood, but of respect and joy in each other's life.
Rarely do members of one family grow up under the same roof.
RICHARD BACH

196
DAYS OLD

DATE:

notes

By seven months of age your baby may begin to cut some teeth. The two lower central incisors may appear, followed by the two front top teeth (upper central incisors).

By about this time (six to seven months of age), you may notice your baby becoming more forceful and bold in biting and mouthing. (Is it all that pent-up crib rage?)

During baby's first year, play is solitary or one-sided. Even so, play helps her learn about the world by stimulating her senses and promoting her movement.

Week 28 ends

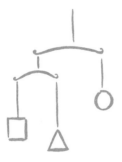

The most remarkable thing about my mother is that for thirty years she served the family nothing but leftovers. The original meal has never been found.

CALVIN TRILLIN

197 DAYS OLD	DATE:

198 DAYS OLD	DATE:

P During months seven through twelve, your baby will probably gain weight at half the rate he did during his first six months. Instead of gaining 1½ pounds (.7 kg) each month, the average monthly weight gain may be closer to ¾ pound (.34 kg).

C Now that your baby is seven months old, she may begin to have more capacity to investigate her environment. By this time, she can probably hold an item in each hand for more than a few seconds. She may also be able to use her fingers to rake at small objects, and she may bang on nearby surfaces (the floor, the cat, your foot . . .).

S As your baby becomes increasingly uncomfortable around others, he may become more clingy and dependent. This behavior is not a sign of weakness or lack of courage as much as it is an affirmation of the secure attachment he feels to you. In order to help the baby through this phase, allow him to cling to mother and father and avoid long separations from him if possible.

P Your baby will probably grow about ½ inch (1.27 cm) in height between now and eight months of age.

C By about seven months or so, babies can usually demonstrate expectation based on what their caregiver says or does. For example, if you tickle your baby after saying "I'm going to get you!" she may scrunch up or start to wiggle in anticipation when she hears the words.

S Clinging, proximity-seeking behavior is healthy, desirable, and necessary. It allows parents to reassure the infant of their presence. With maturity, your baby will realize that you are not going to disappear altogether. Talking to the infant when leaving the room, allowing him to hear your voice over the telephone, and using transitional objects, such as a favorite blanket or toy, help reassure baby of his parent's continued presence.

Check This Out If you're playing a game with baby that she enjoys, she might be laughing and excited; if she doesn't, she might fuss and try to avoid you. Take the hint—baby's not always ready to play when you are.

A hare meeting a lioness one day said reproachfully, "I have always a great number of children, while you have but one or two now and then." The lioness replied, "It is true, but my one child is a lion."

LOKMAN, ETHIOPIAN FABULIST

199 DAYS OLD

DATE:

200 DAYS OLD

DATE:

P At about this time, seven months of age, your baby may be able to sit erect momentarily by leaning forward and bearing weight on both of his hands. This developmental milestone is the cornerstone of many physical and cognitive accomplishments.

C Your baby is beginning to understand that something that disappears from view—a toy, a parent—continues to exist. This insight is called *object permanence*.

S The best way to manage a mobile baby is to combine baby-proofing with distraction: Divert her attention from an area or object by physically moving her to a different location and giving her something she *can* play with.

notes

_____

_____

_____

_____

_____

_____

_____

_____

_____

_____

_____

_____

P When your baby began to make stepping movements, you held him under his arms for support as the steps propelled him forward. Now you're coming into a time when your baby may begin to make stepping movements with you holding his hands instead of his body for support.

C Your baby may begin to respond to the language of a request—just the words—without gestures or other cues. Common reactions include waving in response to "bye-bye"; clapping in reply to "patty-cake"; and pointing or looking in the right direction when asked, "Where's the doggy?"

S The use of a firm voice, eye contact, and a startle, like clapping one's hands loudly, are recommended over the use of physical punishment like spanking or slapping hands during infancy because nothing is gained by its use. Consider this strategy:

1. get baby's attention
2. state the issue (e.g., "We don't touch the plant.")
3. remove the child from the area
4. redirect the child's interest

Did You Know? The development of object permanence is a milestone accomplishment in your baby's ability to think, reason, and solve problems. It enables her to think about all things, not just those that are physically present.

Tomorrow is now.

ELEANOR ROOSEVELT

<table>
<tr><td>

201
DAYS OLD

DATE:

</td><td>

202
DAYS OLD

DATE:

</td></tr>
</table>

(P) By about the end of this (eighth) month, your baby may be able to pull himself to a standing position with the support of your thumbs. (Can you feel it? Walking is on its way!)

(C) By the time baby is eight months of age, she may begin to show some skill at imitating actions that involve eye-hand coordination.

(S) Babies (children and adults, too) sometimes misbehave just to get attention. Consider a milder rebuke and giving positive attention to any behavior you want to encourage. ("I'm glad you are playing so nicely, but these cords are a no-no. They're dangerous. Let's move over here instead.")

(P) Growth in your baby's head circumference slows to a rate about half that experienced during the first six months. Now the average monthly increase is about ¼ inch (.64 cm).

(C) Sometimes a baby who regularly sleeps through the night begins to waken abruptly, perhaps because of a nightmare. Parents are encouraged to check on the baby immediately, but are cautioned to keep reassurances brief to avoid any routine that might perpetuate nighttime waking.

(S) It's often difficult for parents to find time for each other when their baby is an infant because of the responsibilities of raising a family. Positive together time is essential—the happier parents are with each other and their relationship, the more positive the home environment for the baby (at all ages, not just during infancy).

IMPORTANT Remember to show your baby the most attention when he is behaving appropriately, rather than when he is crying or misbehaving. In short, catch him being "good."

Check This Out Play this game with your baby: Place a small cube in a cup and then take it out and hand it to her. By gesture and word (and repeated demonstrations if necessary), encourage the baby to put it in the cup. Even if she places the cube over the cup and doesn't release it, it's still clear that she understood the action.

What is an adult? A child blown up by age.
SIMONE DE BEAUVOIR

203
DAYS OLD

DATE:

_P_ By around this time (seven to eight months) of age), your baby may begin to bring her hands together at the midline of her body, particularly when she is holding a toy in each hand.

_C_ One way to interact with a baby the age of yours is to provide names for the objects and items in his world—parts of the body, toys, animals, people, and foods. (Pointing to yourself and saying "Pooped-out" may not be specific enough.) Frequently repeating those names helps your baby build a vocabulary that he will actually start pronouncing after his first birthday.

_S_ When you are with your baby, describe your actions as though you are reading to her. The narrative provides an interesting commentary and invites her to participate by reacting or just listening.

Week 29 ends

You are either part of the problem or part of the solution.

ELDRIDGE CLEAVER

| 204 DAYS OLD | DATE: | 205 DAYS OLD | DATE: |

P The resistance that babies the age of yours begin to show places them at risk for falling from a changing table, bed, or couch. Never leave your baby unattended, and if he is strong enough to resist restraining, dress and change him on the floor.

C Babies the age of yours (seven to eight months of age), might enjoy playing with a ball of yarn or a wad of sticky tape.

S Some babies fight going to bed and refuse to go to sleep. Bedtime resistance often results from an inconsistent bedtime or too much napping. Evaluate the baby's sleep needs and establish a consistent before-bedtime routine and a predictable bedtime hour.

Check This Out Play this game with your baby: Hold two small toys (cubes or spoons), one in each hand, and bang them together. Offer the toys to your baby and invite her to do the same. What does she do?

P Check the temperature of everything your baby is exposed to—from his bathwater and formula to the sidewalks outside and space heaters. The goal is no burns.

C To stimulate your baby's sense of touch, let your infant play with pieces of fabric or with toys with different textures and surfaces—shiny, smooth, nubby, rippled, squishy, and so on.

S Sometimes a baby will fall asleep in a place other than her own bed. If baby awakens upon transfer and wants to go through her bedtime ritual, parents can certainly accommodate her.

notes

I would rather be a coward than brave because people hurt you when you are brave.

E. M. FORSTER (AS A SMALL CHILD)

2o6 DAYS OLD	DATE:

2o7 DAYS OLD	DATE:

Ⓟ Some children show minimal evidence of teething, such as drooling, increased finger sucking, or biting on hard objects. Others are very irritable and uncomfortable, have trouble sleeping, and refuse to eat. Even without teeth, babies still bite and chew. (That means you can be bitten—gummed?—by a toothless baby.)

Ⓒ Other tactile activities include letting your your baby "catch" running water and splash or lay on his stomach in a large bathtub with shallow water. (Remember to supervise constantly. A baby can drown in any amount of water.)

Ⓢ If your baby was typically smiling and happy at age two months, she should continue to be so now that she's seven months old.

Ⓟ By the time your baby is eight months old, he may begin to transfer an object from one hand to another. This action is more than just the free hand touching the object by chance; it is a deliberate, coordinated action.

Ⓒ Consistency is one of the most important elements of effective discipline. If hitting by the baby is a no-no, then every time she hits, both you and the baby should know what's next—some type of corrective action.

Ⓢ If your baby's mood was generally negative at two months of age, he may tend to cry, fuss, or complain more now at seven to eight months of age.

Every child born into this world belongs to the whole human race.
GREER GARSON

2 0 8 DAYS OLD DATE:

2 0 9 DAYS OLD DATE:

P Spanking is not recommended as discipline for children under the age of two. Babies' heads are large relative to their bodies and a spank with some force behind it can cause a whiplash effect. After the age of two—if parents like to spank—two open-handed swats to the bottom are probably okay. No slapping or hitting about the head—*ever*—because of its potential for lasting harm.

C Sometimes your baby may resist going to bed because of fears. Keep an energy-efficient nightlight on and put her to bed when she's tired. If she wakes during the night, calmly reassure her.

S Your seven- to eight-month-old baby may delight you by laughing aloud for no particular reason. (Maybe he finally got one of your jokes!)

P By seven months of age, your baby may be able to hold an object in one hand while reaching for another object with his other hand. (Baby becomes a consumer!)

C You might begin to pair words with the activities they describe so that baby can begin to learn by association. For example, when you pick your baby up, say "up," and when you put her down, say "down."

S Sometimes children seem to want the parent physically present as they go to sleep. Holding and rocking baby to sleep or taking baby into the parent's bed to fall asleep can be soothing and comforting, but these habits also tend to lead baby to expect that these activities are part of the bedtime routine.

And my parents finally realize that I'm kidnapped and they snap into action immediately:
They rent out my room.

WOODY ALLEN

2 I O
DAYS OLD

DATE:

P In order to reduce the need for nighttime feedings, try to keep your baby awake during meals so that she may learn to associate going to sleep with going to bed rather than with feeding.

C You may notice your baby becoming more of an active agent in getting what he wants, both from the environment in general and from the people around him. Initiative is encouraged by intention, and, increasingly, baby has a plan or purpose in mind and can map out a behavioral strategy.

S As your baby becomes more engrossed during play, she may enjoy exploring the moveable parts of toys.

Week 30 ends

Only love can be divided endlessly and still not diminish.

ANNE MORROW LINDBERGH

2 1 1	DATE:
DAYS OLD	

2 1 2	DATE:
DAYS OLD	

P Install a safety gate at the tops of all staircases, even two-step ones. Any fall will usually be headfirst!

C You might notice your seven- to eight-month-old baby beginning to respond to simple commands, like "open" during feeding, "here" to draw his attention, and "you do it" to help with the bottle.

S While your baby knows you are a source of sustenance, she may also realize that you can facilitate much more. For example, without you to interact with and get toys, some of baby's social goals cannot be achieved.

P When you're playing with your baby, see if he can copy how to clap his hands, bang a drum, push a ball, or perform any other large-muscle skills.

C Babies this age increasingly engage in activities in order to get anticipated results. Notice the types of activities your baby repeats and see if she seems to expect certain outcomes.

S As intention and early goal-directed behavior begin to develop on the baby's part, he—not his parents—will increasingly set the tone of their shared interactions. A parent might think, "Baby has to learn that he doesn't win—I need to win." But infant-directed initiative isn't about competition—it's simply about the human need to make things happen.

One of the virtues of being very young is that you don't let the facts get in the way of your imagination.

SAM LEVENSON

notes

213
DAYS OLD

DATE:

P Even now at seven months of age, your baby may be able to demonstrate increasingly better balance and body control. For example, she can probably begin to raise her chest and upper abdomen off a flat surface, balancing body weight with one hand and arm while exploring with the other. (A one-armed push up! Now you try it!)

C Stimulate your baby's vision and muscle movement by offering her various colored blocks. You can hand them one at a time or demonstrate certain activities with them, like stacking the blocks or lining them up.

S If your baby tended to wake and feed at unpredictable times at two months of age, her feeding and sleep patterns may continue to vary now at seven months old.

The miracle is this—the more we share, the more we have.

LEONARD NIMOY

2 1 4
DAYS OLD

DATE:

2 1 5
DAYS OLD

DATE:

(P) A new reflex—the *parachute reflex*—actually appears for the first time by about seven months (see below). It's possible that this reflex might provide some protection against injuries from a fall.

(C) You may notice that your baby is just beginning to make increased use of his thumb and forefinger in precise opposition when reaching and grasping.

(S) It's important to respect the limits of your child's comfort zone around unfamiliar adults. If she starts climbing, shaking, staring, frowning, or whatever her unique response is, take steps to protect her rather than leaving her exposed. Remember that from baby's point of view, just because people are family doesn't mean they're familiar.

Check This Out See if your baby can demonstrate the parachute reflex: Hold baby horizontally with his stomach parallel to the floor (in a Superman position). Now (carefully) quickly lower the baby downward and see if his hands and fingers automatically extend forward.

(P) By about this time—seven months of age— your baby may begin to pull her head forward in an attempt to sit up by herself.

(C) Read to your baby from books with rhymes and colorful pictures.

(S) As baby approaches eight months of age, he may begin to take more delight in interactive frolic play—the exuberant kinetic romp whereby you become the human swing or you hold the baby above you on extended arms. (If baby is teething, you may have to duck some drool!)

2 1 6
DAYS OLD

DATE:

(P) Your baby's self-feeding skills usually just begin to develop right about now—when your baby is seven months old. You may notice baby wanting to hold her bottle or beginning to hold and play with a spoon during feeding.

(C) Offer your baby a string of big beads, snap-together toys, and simple take-apart toys. These toys can help your baby practice doing and undoing an action.

(S) By the time your baby is eight months old, he may consistently respond to his own name.

Check This Out Here are some ideas for finger foods for baby: soft cooked veggie strips, strips or slices of ripe fruit, toast squares, soft tortillas, and cheese cubes. Use organic foods whenever they're available.

Children have more need of models than of critics.
CAROLYN COATS

notes

_____

<table>
<tr><td>217
DAYS OLD</td><td>DATE:</td></tr>
</table>

P In a few weeks (by the time your baby is about eight months old), she may be able to sit alone, leaning forward on her hands for support.

C Listen when your baby babbles, reproducing consonant-vowel combinations such as "gagaga." Your baby can vocalize this way because she can retain a memory of the sound and remembers how to reproduce it physically.

S You may notice your baby displaying more and more discomfort around unfamiliar people and increasing anxiety when a caregiver leaves the room.

Week 31 ends

In the little world in which children have their existence, whosoever brings them up,
there is nothing so finely perceived and so finely felt as injustice.

CHARLES DICKENS

218 DAYS OLD   DATE:

Ⓟ Sometime between seven and nine months of age, your baby may begin to drink through a straw. This skill is a refinement of the sucking reflex she was born with.

Ⓒ When you and baby read picture books together, try to attract his attention by pointing and saying, "Look! See the____." This training builds an interest in books and pictures, develops his vocabulary, and helps him recognize that pictures of dogs (for instance) can be found in a number of places.

Ⓢ By about eight months of age, your baby may begin to resist having her diaper changed. Make sure your grasp is firm—infants can be as slippery as little fish!

219 DAYS OLD   DATE:

Ⓟ Around this time, your baby's also working on drinking from a cup with your help.

Ⓒ Stimulate your baby's vision and hearing by offering the baby some type of musical toy that moves or lights up.

Ⓢ Babies who resist having their diapers changed also may begin to resist getting dressed. (Maybe you're violating their fashion sense!)

220 DAYS OLD   DATE:

Ⓟ Sometime around eight months of age, your baby may begin to practice lowering herself from a standing position to a sitting position as an intentional act—not a fall—with or without support.

Ⓒ The expression of four basic emotions—pleasure, displeasure, eagerness, and satisfaction or pride—is generally well established by the time your baby is eight months old.

Ⓢ In addition to being able to use vocalizations to express emotion, your baby may begin to use her utterances to add emphasis to something—like indicating that that was really yummy food or a really fun game.

Did You Know? How can infants make their emotions known? They can squeal, scream, kick, pant, hum, or make high-pitched repetitive sounds.

Loving a child doesn't mean giving in to all his whims; to love him is to bring out the best in him, to teach him to love what is difficult.

NADA BOULANGER

221
DAYS OLD

DATE:

222
DAYS OLD

DATE:

Ⓟ Stimulate your baby's hearing by playing any type of music—they're easy at this age—while they are playing, feeding, or resting. They tend to be more interested in vocal music than instrumental music.

Ⓒ By about seven to eight months of age, your baby may be able to consistently pursue and recover nearby toys he has dropped while playing.

Ⓢ Remember that infants the age of yours are still at the height of their stranger stress. Consequently, infants who enter daycare now have more difficulty adjusting than those who enter either earlier or later.

notes

Ⓟ By the end of this eighth month, your baby may begin to creep—to move around on her stomach by kicking her legs and pulling her body with her arms. (It's sort of like boogie boarding without the board.)

Ⓒ Your seven- to eight-month-old baby may be able to consistently turn her head to follow when an object she was playing with (such as a metal spoon) falls noisily to the floor.

Ⓢ You can support any adjustment your baby has to make—change daycare, move to a new house, mom or dad working a different shift, and so on—by being patient, warm, responsive, and flexible. If those qualities don't come to you naturally, practice consciously cultivating them by observing and imitating those traits in others.

Check This Out Play this game with your baby: Let the baby play with a rattle or other toy for a short time while he is lying on his back in the crib. Gently take it from him and place it on his chest or beside his shoulder within easy reach. Does he pursue it?

The word no *carries a lot more meaning when spoken by a parent who also knows how to say* yes.
JOYCE MAYNARD

2 2 3
DAYS OLD

DATE:

2 2 4
DAYS OLD

DATE:

P While baby practices pulling himself to a standing position with the support of your thumbs, he should be much better at pulling himself to a sitting position while he is lying on his back.

C You may have noticed how comfortably your baby plays with objects that are close to her that she happens to notice. This collection of skills makes play possible—your baby can rotate her wrist; reach with a pincer grasp; hold objects in her hands; examine objects by mouthing, touch, and vision; sit steadily; and move if she has to.

S For the child who is sensitive or frightens easily, a soothing caregiver becomes an important source of support. Soothing a frightened child does not tend to spoil them or reward fearfulness—it just comforts them and makes them feel more at ease in the presence of something perceived as scary or unusual.

P Now that your baby is seven to eight months old, he probably relies on his palm, fingers, *and* his thumb in grasping. The inclusion of the thumb is an important component in overall eye-hand coordination.

C Now that your baby is eight months of age, you can probably see how her mode of exploration has shifted away from mouthing and toward visual and tactile exploration. If you hand your baby a red ring, for example, she may take a multimodal approach: mouthing it, looking at it, and watching it's movement as she manipulates it.

S Another way that your baby learns is by imitation, and babies are eager to imitate others. For example, your baby may enjoy using a cup or plastic glass as he sees others do; he may also begin to imitate the sounds he hears around him.

Week 32 ends

Loving a baby is a circular business, a kind of feedback loop. The more you give the more you get and the more you feel like giving.

PENELOPE LEACH

225 DAYS OLD

DATE:

P A baby who can sit in a baby activity center can have tons of fun.

C By about this time (eight to nine months of age), you'll probably notice that your baby is getting better and better at using one object to retrieve another.

S Babies who are easily frustrated benefit from patience and flexibility. (Don't we all!)

226 DAYS OLD

DATE:

P A ride on a baby swing will engage your baby's sense of balance and motion. Be safe.

C Your baby may begin to add the consonants *t*, *d*, and *w* to her vocalizations. Syllable combinations such as "dada" or "mama" may be heard, but your baby may not ascribe meaning to them for a few more months.

S For a baby who seeks excitement, a caregiver can become an important source of fun. You'll probably find that anything you do with a smile and playful tone in your voice will delight your baby, if he's in the mood for fun.

Babies are beautiful, wonderful, exciting, enchanting, extraordinary little creatures—who grow up into ordinary folk like us.
DORIS DYSON

227 DAYS OLD	DATE:

228 DAYS OLD	DATE:

P Sometime between eight and nine months of age, your baby may begin to show regular patterns in bowel and bladder habits. (That's a development that will make you feel flushed with joy!)

C Babies the age of yours may spontaneously vocalize in a variety of settings and situations. For example, she may "talk" to her toys and to her image in the mirror.

S By about eight months of age, your baby may become much more likely to repeat activities that are followed by positive attention, such as laughter, cheering, hugging, and clapping. This development provides an insight into how powerful training by reward can be.

P By about nine months of age, your baby may be able to sit steadily on the floor for a prolonged period of time.

C Offer your baby books with cutouts and interesting attachments such as a zipper or a handle.

S As early as nine months of age, if an infant's game (like peek-a-boo or "where's your nose?") is interrupted, she is more likely to remember the game and want to get back to it than when she was younger and more distractible.

notes

_____

_____

_____

_____

_____

_____

_____

_____

_____

_____

_____

_____

Feelings are everywhere—be gentle.

J. MASAI

229 DAYS OLD · DATE:

230 DAYS OLD · DATE:

P By about nine months of age, your baby may be able to hold a block by using his thumb and index finger in an immature version of the pincer grasp.

C Infants do not usually generate new behaviors to accomplish goals. Instead, they typically try out existing strategies—like poking, mouthing, shaking, pulling, et cetera—to solve problems.

S By about nine months, the emotional range of an infant includes a desire to be physically close to caregivers. For example, your baby might want to be picked up a lot or she might hug back when hugged. (Those little arms around your neck feel like heaven!)

P By the time your baby is nine months old, he may be able to control his balance well enough to reach up in the air for an object while staying seated.

C At about eight to nine months of age, infants can begin to recognize the names of people they know or favorite toys. Your baby might indicate comprehension by turning her head toward or reaching for the named object or person.

S Your nine-month-old baby may be able to initiate activities that bring about pleasure and excitement. For example, your baby might smile playfully and vocalize joyfully while putting his finger into the caregiver's mouth or offering his rattle for the caregiver to mouth.

Did You Know? The pincer grasp is a key element of fine motor coordination.

If you judge people, you have no time to love them.
MOTHER TERESA

2 3 1
DAYS OLD

DATE:

P By about eight months of age, your baby may begin to creep or crawl on her stomach or hands because of a reflex that helps her draw her knees to her chest when placed face down. (And the correct question is: What is the tonic-labyrinthine reflex?)

C Between now and your baby's first birthday, your baby may begin to be curious about objects that seem to be associated with different objects, like a bead hidden in a box.

S Sometime around nine months of age, your baby may begin to imitate an action he's never performed (like the action of sticking out his tongue) or is unable to see (like the action of touching an ear).

Week 33 ends

Nothing great was ever achieved without enthusiam.

RALPH WALDO EMERSON

Week 34 Begins

DATE:

2 3 2
DAYS OLD

DATE:

2 3 3
DAYS OLD

℗ By this time (eight to nine months of age), if not before, move your baby into a full-size crib and lower the mattress completely. This will keep her safer when she pulls herself to a standing position.

© You may have noticed that your baby enjoys the sensation of movement. He probably enjoys going for a walk in the stroller, being pulled in a wagon, or being carried.

§ Within the next few weeks—by about nine months—your baby may be relatively more responsive to her caregiver's voice, facial expressions, and touch and much less responsive to the attention of others, particularly people she doesn't know.

Check This Out Play this game with your baby: Place two beads (or any comparable item) into a small box without a lid and gently rattle the box. Then empty the beads onto the table in front of baby and immediately return the beads to the box and shake it again. Then, while holding the box outside the child's field of vision, remove the beads and give her the empty box. Take back the box and repeat the whole process, but this time leave the beads in the box when you give it to your child. What does she do? Is she looking for the beads in the box?

℗ By about nine months of age, your baby can begin to use her fingers as a unit to sweep a small object (like a Cheerio) into her palm. (In the United States, Cheerios have been a veritable infant institution since 1941.)

© At about nine months, your infant may be more tolerant of bright lights than she was at an earlier age and less sensitive to loud but familiar sounds, like the roar of the vacuum cleaner or the flush of the toilet. Her nervous system is getting used to things.

§ You may notice that by about nine months of age, your baby may begin to hold his caregiver's hand when being touched or tickled.

To touch a child's face, a dog's smooth coat, a petaled flower, the rough surface of a rock
is to set up new orders of brain motion. To touch is to communicate.

JAMES W. ANGELL

234 DAYS OLD	DATE:

235 DAYS OLD	DATE:

P All the playing your baby does tires her out. Between eight and nine months of age, she'll probably be taking two naps a day of one to two hours each, and she'll usually sleep through most of the night.

C Your baby's perception of the boundaries of his own body are improving. He may begin to notice, look at, or attempt to touch a toy that is placed on part of his body, like his stomach, head, or leg.

S One of the things a nine-month-old baby may begin to do is initiate exploration, as when a baby touches and explores her caregiver's mouth or ear.

P By about nine months of age, your baby may be able to transfer objects from one hand to the other and put objects (like blocks) into a container (like a box or a bucket) and take them out again. (Ah . . . the first signs of being able to clean up?)

C By about nine months of age, your baby can probably vocalize different sounds that form in the front of his mouth, like "ba," "da," and "ma."

S Your nine-month-old-baby may begin to protest and express anger. For example, she might scream when she doesn't get the toy she wants or push food she doesn't want off her tray with an angry look.

The way I see it, if you want the rainbow, you gotta put up with the rain.
DOLLY PARTON

notes

236
DAYS OLD

DATE:

P A typical behavior of a child between eight and nine months of age is to bang her toys or her hands while playing.

C Now that she can rotate her wrist, your baby can better understand the concept of right-side up and up-side down.

S By about nine months, your baby may express fear—especially in the presence of strangers—by turning away, looking scared, or crying when a stranger approaches too quickly or too closely.

Check This Out Play this game with your baby: Select an item (like a footed cup) that has a clear up and down side. Turn the cup over and say, "Down." Then turn it back and say, "Up." When you repeat the demonstration close by your baby, what does he do? Does he rotate his wrist to turn the cup?

The toughest thing about raising kids is convincing them that you have seniority.
ANONYMOUS

237 DAYS OLD	DATE:

238 DAYS OLD	DATE:

P By around eight months or so, your baby may be able to raise herself in an effort to sit up when placed on her back. In due time, those world-class abs will also help her flip over, crawl, and pull herself to standing.

C By about this time, your baby may begin to engage in cause-and-effect playing. This type of play seems focused on exploring a toy with the question: "What will happen when I throw it/pull it/wear it/hold it far from me/bring it in close/press it down . . ." The possibilities are endless.

S Between nine and eleven months of age, the emotional range of infants may include responding to the caregiver's gestures with an intentional gesture of his own, such as waving his arm or blowing a kiss.

P While your own baby may be toothless (no worries), if a baby's two lower-middle incisors have erupted, the next pair may be the two upper-middle incisors.

C Most eight- to nine-month-old babies can begin to recall past events and give evidence of memory through their behavior. For example, if your baby recognizes a disliked food, she might shake her head or close her mouth tightly in order to avoid another bad experience.

S Your nine-month-old baby may have the capacity to react to an affectionate vocalization and facial expression by offering a playful look and a series of vocalizations in response. (Love reciprocated.)

Week 34 ends

notes

_____
_____
_____
_____
_____
_____
_____
_____
_____

All we are is the result of what we have thought.

BUDDHA

239 DAYS OLD

DATE:

240 DAYS OLD

DATE:

P By about eight months of age, your baby may begin to creep or crawl on his stomach or hands, possibly progressing backward at first. Pushing with the better-developed arms may be easier for him than pulling forward with his arms or pushing with his knees.

C By about nine months, you may notice your baby showing interest in new toys by carefully examining them.

S In general, the more cues that accompany an expressed emotion from a caregiver, the more intensely baby tends to react. For example, if mothers express emotions like joy both facially and vocally, their babies tend to watch them longer, play more, and respond more happily than babies whose mothers express joy only facially.

P By about eight to nine months of age, your baby may begin to work on bending her knees so she can stand up and then sit down. (Those short little legs are so cute!)

C Your baby may demonstrate more and more sophisticated problem solving. For example, by nine months, your baby may begin to pull on a rug, towel, or corner of a blanket to bring an out-of-reach object closer.

S Babies tend to turn their eyes away and show more sadness and anger when their mothers express emotions like sadness both facially and vocally. For emotional validity, caregivers need to walk the walk and talk the talk. Inconsistency confuses infants.

If help and salvation are to come, they can only come from children, for children are the makers of men.

MARIA MONTESSORI

241
DAYS OLD

DATE:

242
DAYS OLD

DATE:

P Because babies can climb stairs, place gates at both the top and bottom of stairs in case your baby has access at either end. Keep all doors to the outside (including pet doors) closed and locked.

C Your baby may be able to demonstrate that he can tell the difference between people and animals by displaying different responses. For example, he may kick with joy when he sees his mother, but put a hand out for a lick when he sees the dog. (Or vice versa!)

S Your baby's vocalizations now may deliberately contain sounds to convey emotions such as pleasure and satisfaction.

P By around nine months of age, toe play when barefoot may replace hand play as your baby explores the world beyond her fingertips.

C By about nine months of age, your baby may be able to imitate a few sounds, such as sniffs, clicks, a cough, blowing sounds like exhaling, or a "raspberry." (You can bet your little copycat is watching for your reaction when she does!)

S By about nine months of age, the baby may feel emotionally closer to the caregiver (especially the mother) and seem to show increasing interest in pleasing her parent.

IMPORTANT Infant mobility increases safety concerns. Baby-proof your home and always use line-of-sight supervision!

Love Notes Want to promote the development of a positive self-image? Respond positively to baby's overtures to please you.

You must first get along with yourself before you can get along with others.
ANTHONY J. D'ANGELO

243 DAYS OLD	DATE:

244 DAYS OLD	DATE:

P Your baby may be able to grasp another 1-inch (2.5-cm) cube even if he is holding two others. (Early training for clearance sales.)

C Your baby's ability to tell the difference between similar sounds and to select specific vocalizations and behaviors as responses is improving. For example, baby might respond by saying "ooooo" when her caregiver imitates the woof, woof sound of a dog. But when she notices the family dog, she might say "dah-dah."

S Babies are generally able to respond to their name and understand simple directions like "Come here" and "No, no"—by about nine months of age.

Check This Out Play this game with your baby: Place a cube in each of your baby's hands. Offer him a third cube or place it along with one of the other cubes in baby's hand. What does he do to try to accommodate so many toys?

P By about nine months of age, your baby's balance is improved but not perfected. Your baby can probably recover her balance when she leans forward, but usually cannot do so when leaning sideways.

C Within the next few weeks, your baby may begin to tilt his head diagonally and directly toward a sound source to better fix its location.

S Around nine months of age, your baby may begin to communicate intentionally with caregivers and others. The development of this phase of intentional communication ends with the production of baby's first words around baby's first birthday.

notes

For unflagging interest and enjoyment, [I recommend] a housefold of children. If things go reasonably well, certainly all other forms of success and achievement lose their importance by comparison.

THEODORE ROOSEVELT

245
DAYS OLD

DATE:

P Sometime between eight and ten months of age, your baby may begin to pull herself to a standing position if she can hold on to someone or something for support. What's more, she may venture forth—Make Way for Baby! (*Make Way for Ducklings* is a charming book.)

C The mechanism that helps your baby see the world in three dimensions is more mature at nine months of age, so baby's depth perception and ability to judge distance is improving. (Unfortunately, this doesn't mean that baby will be more cautious; and if he's a little thrill-seeker, just the opposite.)

S Your baby may also be generally involved in deliberate attention-seeking behavior and intentional problem solving.

Did You Know? Intentional behavior is the hallmark of a baby between eight and twelve months of age.

Week 35 ends

The supreme happiness of life is the conviction that we are loved.
VICTOR HUGO

<table>
<tr><td>246 DAYS OLD</td><td>DATE:</td></tr>
</table>

246 DAYS OLD DATE:

247 DAYS OLD DATE:

(P) If you and your baby do read or look at picture books together, she may begin to turn the pages of a cloth book or a board book on her own. The behavior may be clumsy at first, but it should be well established by her first birthday!

(C) By about nine months, your baby may begin to notice the texture of objects. Happily, there are lots of books that make it easy and fun to discover some of the nuances of texture.

(S) One strategy your baby may use to help attract the attention of others is simply to shout. ("Yo! Over here!")

(P) By about nine months, you may notice that your baby seems to demonstrate a preference for using a dominant hand.

(C) Intentional behavior involves carrying out a preconceived plan on purpose, not by accident. This approach is so different from when he was younger and things happened almost by chance.

(S) Your baby's attempts to communicate might include reacting to something new, a behavioral response to a request or question, and protesting something she doesn't want to do.

Did You Know? Handedness doesn't seem to follow any regular pattern of inheritance, so it's entirely likely that a left-handed baby might be born to right-handed parents and vice versa.

Children's talent to endure stems from their ignorance of alternatives.
MAYA ANGELOU

248 DAYS OLD	DATE:

249 DAYS OLD	DATE:

By about nine months of age, your baby is able to bring two objects together—one in each hand—for a visual comparison. (Or simply to bang them together!)

One type of intentional problem solving involves applying a known approach to a new situation. For example, if uncovering a hidden toy reveals the toy, then taking the paper off wrapped gifts (even if it's not time to do so) should reveal what's inside the boxes.

Between nine and twelve months of age, your baby's behavior may indicate that she is expecting or waiting for a response from an adult. For example, your baby may look at an adult, point to an object that is on a shelf too high to reach, and then look "expectantly" at the adult. (And if nothing happens, you remember the banging we just talked about? *Lots* of that.)

notes

_____

_____

_____

_____

_____

_____

_____

_____

_____

Do not give your baby peanut butter until he is about a year old, since he cannot chew it thoroughly (even the creamy kind) and might choke. It also has high allergic potential.

By about this time (eight to nine months of age), you'll probably notice that baby is getting better and better at using one object to act on another. For example, she might push away an obstacle to get to an object or pull a string to obtain the object attached to it.

Your baby has had eight months to investigate the toys and other objects he has access to, and there are probably some toys he likes better than others. Since being able to assert himself is becoming more important, try to offer him at least two toys to play with when you're on the go. Then he has choice, but within your limits.

Check This Out Play this game with your baby: Put a small toy in the middle of your hand and then close your fingers around it. What does your baby do?

Never lend your car to anyone you gave birth to.

MILTON BERLE

2 5 0 DAYS OLD	DATE:

2 5 1 DAYS OLD	DATE:

(P) By now (about nine months of age), your baby may be able to rotate her trunk while sitting unsupported. Trunk rotation will also help your baby turn around when she's crawling. (If Chuck Berry would say, "Come on, baby. Let's do the Twist," your baby could!)

(C) Infants may also enlist the help of others by having the person who first produced the event repeat it. For example, baby might put a whistle into his mother's mouth to be blown again or place his father's hand against a toy that he wants activated.

(S) A securely attached baby loves to be around her caregivers. Often, it seems, she just can't get enough of them. At nine months of age, that balance begins to tip ever so slowly as baby's motivation to be with you is trumped by her motivation to leave your lap and explore her world. There is one major requirement, however: You can't leave baby's line of sight, because sooner or later, she'll want to check back in with you.

(P) Some of your baby's favorite toys will be kitchen utensils, bowls, and pots and pans. For safety's sake, offer baby the items (if any) before she learns how to open doors and drawers to find them.

(C) By about nine months of age, your baby may begin to persist in his attempts to communicate, even if he was unsuccessful the first time. For example, if the person he's speaking to doesn't respond when he points to what he wants, he might modify the original message by adding jumping up and down or tugging on the person's clothing.

(S) When you are with your baby, provide a narration that describes what's going on. For example, "Let's walk to the table to find our book. Here it is—it has a bear family on the cover. We'll sit right down on this chair. . . ." It's like being a play-by-play announcer for baseball or softball—slow and easy. Not ice hockey.

IMPORTANT Childproof all your drawers and cabinets, even the ones you think baby will never reach!

Children find everything in nothing; men find nothing in everything.
GIACOMO LEOPARDI

252
DAYS OLD

DATE:

notes

(P) Looking back on the last thirty days, a typical baby is expected to be 12 to 20 ounces (340 to 567 g) heavier, about ½ inch (1.3 cm) taller, and ¼ inch (0.6 cm) larger in head circumference.

(C) Even though she can't speak yet, your baby still understands much of what you say. Like anyone learning a new language, her ability to comprehend outstrips (at this age, nearly completely) her ability to express herself. And she watches how you say it.

(S) Even though you might think you have the emotions you're struggling with under control, you will still give yourself away to your baby. He's starting to evaluate his caregiver's moods by studying facial cues, tone of voice, and the way he's handled. Right now, babies are emotional sponges. When we're happy, so are they; and when we're not, they aren't either. Food for thought.

Week 36 ends

Children are all foreigners. We treat them as such. We cannot understand their speech or mode of life, and so our education is remote and accidental and not closely applied to the facts.

RALPH WALDO EMERSON

253 DAYS OLD	DATE:

254 DAYS OLD	DATE:

P By about this time (nine to ten months of age), your baby may be able to stand holding on to furniture and possibly even to pull herself to a standing position, but she may not be able to get back down except by falling.

C By about nine months of age, your baby's capacity to focus attention increases to include, for example, both the caregiver who is reading the story and the pictures in the story book.

S By nine months of age, babies may begin to try harder to control the amount of attention they are able to direct toward a task. The ability to concentrate, maintain focus, and avoid distraction takes years to develop, but it begins right here—in infancy.

P By nine or ten months, your baby may be able to release an object in his hand by pressing it against a firm surface.

C Your nine- to ten-month-old is working on developing the ability to anticipate what's going to happen next on the basis of a cue. For example, when she's put in the car seat, your baby learns that that means she will be buckled in to go bye-bye. Also, when you approach her with a tissue in your hand, she learns it's time to blow her nose. (You may also see some fast moves and tricky behavior as she tries to avoid the encounter!)

S If a problem needs to be solved—a jacket put on or a container opened—the nine- to ten-month-old baby might simply give the item to someone nearby and hope for some help.

Children are living jewels dropped unstained from heaven.
ROBERT POLLOK

255 DAYS OLD   DATE:

256 DAYS OLD   DATE:

Sometime between now and about thirteen months of age, your baby may begin to stand on his own without any support.

Much of what babies the age of yours do is to use strategies that they are familiar with—like shaking, banging, or squeezing—to explore the characteristics of objects. They will also continue to bring objects to their mouths.

The same message—this container needs to be opened—can be conveyed by looking at the adult, shaking the container, handing it to the adult, and directing an expectant look back toward the adult.

Check This Out How does your baby respond when you place her in a standing position? Make sure she's stable and balanced on her feet, and then remove the support of your hands.

Between now and your baby's first birthday he may begin to take at least three steps without support.

By around this time (nine to ten months of age), your baby may be getting good at imitating new sounds and gestures.

You may have noticed your baby beginning to attach to a blanket, stuffed toy, or other object. An attachment to an inanimate object is common during infancy in part because it is a mobile source of temporary comfort during change or stress.

notes

_____

The child at play is noisy and ought to be noisy: Sir Isaac Newton at work is quiet and ought to be quiet.
And the child should spend most of its time at play, whilst the adult should spend most of his time at work.
GEORGE BERNARD SHAW

257 DAYS OLD	DATE:

258 DAYS OLD	DATE:

P About 72 percent of infants between the ages of nine and twelve months can get six hours of continuous sleep. (That means caregivers can, too!)

C From nine to twelve months of age, the intonation associated with a baby's babbling reflects the contours of *statements* (slowly rising and falling), *requests* (slowly rising and rising again), and *commands* (sharply rising and falling).

S For the most part, babies the age of yours enjoy the predictability of a routine. When changes occur in that routine, attachment objects like blankets and special toys seem to satisfy some of baby's comfort and security needs. Attachment objects may be especially soothing, for example, if you are changing daycare providers or if the family is in the process of moving.

P Between now and your baby's first birthday, the number of feedings from breast or bottle may decrease as baby eats more solid food. She may even begin to eat mashed or chopped food from the family meal.

C By about this time (nine to ten months of age) the sound sequences that your baby produces begins to resemble actual words. This vocalization is called "jabber."

S If your baby has attached to a one-of-a-kind object or special blanket, you may have trouble keeping it from getting soiled and threadbare. You may want to try to find a duplicate toy or blanket in case the original is lost or beyond repair.

Nothing was a stronger influence psychologically on their environment, and especially on their children, than the unlived life of the parents.

CARL JUNG

2 5 9 DAYS OLD

DATE:

P When babies are ill or hurting from teething, they may want their bottle again or to use their bottle more and their sippy cup less. Sucking can relax and comfort them and give teething babies something to bite down on. (If they bite during breast-feeding, take them off the breast right away to communicate "No biting.")

C Sometime between eight and thirteen months of age, your baby may begin to be able to take a lid off a box to uncover a small toy or object.

S It may make sense to try to restrict the use of an attachment object to the car, the house, and daycare. Even so, it's hard to find something that offers sure-fire comfort. You'll know what's best for your particular baby.

Check This Out Play this game with your baby: As your baby watches, place a toy or small object into a box and then cover the box with a solid lid. Open the box and remove the object, then put it back in the box and replace the lid. Hand the closed box to the baby and say, "Can you get the [object]?" and see what she does.

Week 37 ends

We are always too busy for our children; we never give them the time or interest they deserve. We lavish gifts upon them; but the most precious gift, our personal association, which means so much to them, we give grudgingly.

MARK TWAIN

260	DATE:
DAYS OLD	

261	DATE:
DAYS OLD	

P While babies continue to be comforted by sucking, a bottle should probably not be used as a comfort object, especially at night. The milk, juice, or other liquid from the bottle that pools around baby's teeth or drips into baby's ear can attract bacteria and cause tooth decay or ear infection. A pacifier, thumb, stuffed toy, or teething toy may be a better substitute.

C The lidded box game can be a great way to interact. (For variety, put a different item in the box each time.) Almost always, babies the age of yours react with an incredibly sweet blend of raw surprise and excitement upon finding the object, because they're not jaded in any way. They won't telegraph impatience—"I can't believe you put a pacifier in the box! What were you thinking?" Just the opposite. At this point they have fun with *anything* in the box—a rock from the yard, a broken crayon—because *you're* there to share it with them.

S Saying "goodbye" to your baby at daycare is more difficult now that he may be distressed when you leave. Use a succinct exit strategy rather than a prolonged ordeal. It's important that you let him know you're leaving so that it doesn't seem like you're still around but just hidden.

P Allow your baby to practice feeding herself with a spoon.

C Your baby may begin to discover that hiding an object doesn't mean it is gone. This insight marks the beginning of intellectual reasoning.

S Let your baby feel cold objects (like an ice pack) or warm objects (like a towel from the dryer), and tell him what the temperature is.

Check This Out Play this game with your baby: Let her watch an object disappear under a cover and then say, "Where did it go? Where's the toy?" What does your baby do?

The family is one of nature's masterpieces.

GEORGE SANTAYANA

262 DAYS OLD   DATE:

263 DAYS OLD   DATE:

P Sometime between now and your baby's first birthday, your baby may begin to hold his own bottle and drink from it.

C While babies use cues to anticipate what's going to happen to themselves next, they use that same type of learning to anticipate what's up next for others. For example, if your baby sees family members busying to leave, her own activity level may increase. Or, if Daddy says, "Bye-bye," she may understand that he's going to work.

S Your baby may begin to show increasing interest in her mirror image.

notes

_____

_____

_____

_____

_____

_____

_____

_____

_____

_____

_____

_____

P Allow your baby to drink from a sippy cup or a cup with a straw. Even with a lid, there are spills, so keep that paper towel handy.

C Between nine and twelve months of age, your baby may begin to understand the concepts of "in" and "out."

S At first, your baby could pay attention to objects and patterns. Then when one of the patterns morphed into a human face, your baby paid attention to whether that face was familiar. Now at about nine months of age, she recognizes familiar objects, too.

Did You Know? Your baby is working to develop a critical skill—the ability to keep tabs on two things at once and shift attention between the two without losing track of either one. This ability is a fundamental feature of the ability to learn.

Check This Out Play this game with your baby: Gather some blocks or balls and some type of container—a plastic bowl or a cardboard box. Take a toy and place it in the container and let the baby look at it. Say, "In. The block is in." Then give baby his own block and say, "Can you put it in?" After four or so blocks are in the container, retrieve one and say, "Out. This block is out." Then encourage baby to reach for one of the blocks in the box, "Out. Take the block out."

So much of what is best in us is bound up in our love of family, that it remains the measure of our stability because it measures our sense of loyalty. All other pacts of love or fear derive from it and are modeled upon it.

DANIEL LONG

| 264 DAYS OLD | DATE: |

| 265 DAYS OLD | DATE: |

Ⓟ Self-feeding with a spoon is a tough thing to master. Your baby is probably getting more food on herself and her tray than in her mouth! That's okay. Everyone starts out messy.

Ⓒ The infant between nine and twelve months of age can begin to distinguish objects from his related activity and perceive them as objects of his own. For example, even though a high chair is strongly associated with mealtime, it is actually a multipurpose staging area. Baby can touch a kitten, play with stacking toys, or shake his rattle while sitting there.

Ⓢ Boisterous play with surprising movements and touch seem to be most effective in producing laughter in nine- to ten-month-old babies. (And if baby doesn't laugh, you can usually get a chuckle from someone who's watching you!)

Ⓟ By about this time (nine months of age), your baby may be able to sit alone steadily, with his back more straight than curved.

Ⓒ Sometime between nine and thirteen months of age, your baby may be able to place more than one cube into a cup or container.

Ⓢ A baby about the age of yours (nine to ten months) may turn his head toward familiar voices, respond to his name, and show that he recognizes familiar people.

Check This Out Play this game with baby: After your baby has placed one block into a cup, place eight more blocks in front of her and say, "Let's put them all in." Put all the blocks in the cup, urging baby to join you by gesturing to her and/or demonstrating how to do it.

The family is the nucleus of civilization.
WILLIAM JAMES DURANT

266
DAYS OLD

DATE:

notes

P Your baby's ability to use the palm of his hand and his fingers to scoop or rake at items to pick them up is generally well established now that your baby is nine months old.

C Try reading and reciting simple rhymes. Rhymes fascinate baby because of their predictable tempo and repetitive sounds (e.g., "Hickory, dickory dock / the mouse ran up the clock.")

S Depending on the season, you and your baby may enjoy experiencing the coolness of water on a warm, sunny day, the scent of fresh flowers, the fun of the leaf pile in autumn, or the crispness of snow during winter. What a privilege it is to share these first seasons with your baby!

Week 38 ends

Fatherhood is pretending the present you like most is soap-on-a-rope.
BILL COSBY

267 DAYS OLD   DATE:

268 DAYS OLD   DATE:

P In another few weeks—by about ten months—your baby may be able to make stepping movements with you holding her hands for support.

C If something is in your baby's way, he may begin to climb over it or push it away. (When he was younger, an obstacle would encourage him to give up.)

S By about this time (nine to ten months of age) your baby may begin to become proficient at identifying emotions in the facial expressions and vocalizations of others. For example, baby may begin to smile in response to a happy voice and frown in response to an angry voice.

P Through the exercises that involve the placement of objects in cups, bowls, and pegboards, your baby is learning how to operate in the world by imitating your actions and listening to the narration of those events.

C By about six months of age, infants successfully reach and grasp the objects they see about 33 percent of the time. Now, by about nine to ten months of age, this figure improves to upwards of 80 percent. (Watch your wallet!)

S In baby's second six months, you may notice her becoming increasingly alert to mother's activities and whereabouts, particularly if mother is the primary caregiver.

Mothers of daughters are daughters of mothers and have remained so, in circles joined to circles, since time began. They are bound by a shared destiny.

SIGNE HAMMER

269 DAYS OLD

DATE:

270 DAYS OLD

DATE:

P By about eleven months of age, most babies can lower themselves from a standing position to a sitting position without falling. Your baby may take your hand or use a piece of furniture like a handrail for support.

C Jabber (or expressive jargon) mimics the inflections used during conversation and is often accompanied by pointing or some other gesture.

S It's typical for your infant to be more difficult to manage during diapering and dressing at this age. More and more he wants to choose what he does, and that may not include making a hygienic pit stop.

Did You Know? Three important tasks are accomplished by play: Play allows the baby to develop and practice muscle skills; as a social experience, your baby learns how to interact with others and picks up behavior by observation; as a source of information, your baby learns about people, objects, and circumstances.

P By about this time (nine to ten months of age), your baby may begin to bring her hands together at the midline of her body—particularly when she is holding a toy in one or both hands.

C Babies about the age of yours are beginning to learn how to respond to a verbal request, particularly one without an accompanying gesture. Common responses include waving in reply to someone saying "bye-bye," clapping hands in response to the patty-cake rhyme, and pointing or looking in the right direction when asked, "Where is your blanket?" or "Where is your toy bear?"

S Your baby's increased desire for freedom of movement and independence may lessen his need to be held close for feedings. As your baby acquires more control over his actions, he may want to play a bigger role in choosing what he wants to eat and when, for example.

Don't count the days. Make the days count.
MUHAMMAD ALI

notes

271
DAYS OLD

DATE:

When your baby wants to cooperate when being dressed, she can probably begin to extend an arm or leg to help.

In these second six months of infancy, your baby will probably become better and better at conveying his intentions—what he plans to do—through vocalizations.

One activity that you and your baby might share is to investigate how different things move in the wind generated by a fan. (If it's the right season, this suggestion can sound like pure genius!)

The way to love anything is to realize it might be lost.

G. K. CHESTERTON

272 DAYS OLD	DATE:

273 DAYS OLD	DATE:

(P) Babies the age of yours (nine to ten months old) are beginning to learn how to use both hands in a well-coordinated action. For example, he may be able to lift up a cup with one hand and pick up the object hidden under the cup with the other. (Now you see it . . . now you don't.)

(C) In another few weeks—by about ten months—babies begin to actively listen for the speech sounds that form the basic words of their native language. Humans are hardwired to pay more attention to the sounds that have become familiar and less attention to sounds outside of their language.

(S) Even though your baby might be familiar with the word *no*, and she might know that it means to stop what she is doing, she still won't always obey it. It may take another year or so of development for her to become more responsive to prohibitions. (A whole *year?*)

(P) Babies are completely helpless in water. They are also at increased risk for ear infections. Swallowing large amounts of water can result in convulsions. Watch your child at all times.

(C) You may notice that your baby is much more of an active participant when you read together, responding to some of the pictures with interest or recognition. Point at the picture and name it, describe what it looks like, and tell what's going on in short, simple sentences.

(S) As your baby matures, he may begin to rely on you as a source of security for exploration. He may leave to explore, but if he feels uncomfortable, he may come back to the safety of your arms or lap.

Check This Out What conflicts arise for caregivers who are safe bases for their exploring infants? One conflict may involve how much comfort and assistance to provide the baby; another is how much independence should be permitted or encouraged.

Week 39 ends

notes

Never invest in anything that eats or needs repairing.

BILLY ROSE

274 DAYS OLD — DATE:

275 DAYS OLD — DATE:

P — Like bottle-fed babies, breast-fed babies may lose interest in breast-feeding around this time and may regularly pull away from the breast or suck for a very short period of time. Why? Your baby may simply be ready to take calories from other sources because she's increasingly active. On the other hand, the spoon is new and may look interesting, especially if baby knows that good things come from spoons.

C — By about ten months of age, your baby may begin to turn his head and actively look to the floor when he drops a toy.

S — Your baby may become more particular not only about what she eats but when. If food is offered, she will eat only if she's hungry. It doesn't help to make mealtime a battle. A baby who is getting enough to eat is usually energetic, industrious, and making steady developmental progress. And if food is available, another meal is just around the corner.

P — To improve his balance, play this game when your baby is first learning to walk: Place a few small beads or other small toys on the floor. Hold baby's hand as he walks. When he reaches the toys, he will have to lift his foot to step over them and balance momentarily on one foot. Tell him he is stepping over the toy as he walks.

C — Typically, language learners can translate meaning far better than they can express themselves in words. Your baby is no exception. Help her show what she knows by pointing with her, using meaningful gestures, or nodding at her.

S — One inevitable outcome of a curious mobile child with a growing brain is a messy house. Give your baby freedom to play and explore, but baby-proof what you can and set reasonable limits on the types and locations of the messes he can make.

Happiness isn't something you experience; it's something you remember.

OSCAR KEVANT

276
DAYS OLD

DATE:

P Your baby won't develop an arch in his foot yet, even though he may be taking some steps. Barefoot walking helps develop the muscles in baby's feet better than walking in shoes.

C Showing interest in the details of objects is usually well established by now. Babies the age of yours will turn objects in their hands to investigate all parts.

S Your baby can initiate interactions with others by displaying meaningful gestures. Pointing, for instance, may be an announcement of interest, which, when you put into words, might sound like, "That's a big flower, isn't it?"

Sweater, n. A garment worn by a child when its mother feels chilly.

AMBROSE BIERCE

277 DAYS OLD | DATE:

P Pushing a stroller or a small pushcart or any other toy that has a push handle about her size may help your baby develop the balance she needs to be better at walking.

C Creeping and crawling can aid the development of your baby's visual perception. Looking at an object from all sides helps baby recognize the object from any viewing angle.

S Your baby may demonstrate his interest in a person by looking, listening, touching, or moving toward that person.

IMPORTANT Keep large toys and bumper pads out of baby's crib or playpen—he might figure out how to use them as "stairs" and climb out.

278 DAYS OLD | DATE:

P Your baby may not cut her first tooth until her first birthday. How many teeth a baby has and when they appear is unrelated to her ability to think, solve problems, communicate, develop and express emotions, or interact with others.

C Throughout your baby's first year, most everything will be explored by mouthing, sucking, or biting.

S Your baby might seek out warmth and pleasure by using nonverbal cues, such as reaching up for a hug, crawling into your lap, and cuddling closely when held. Baby might also say "Up" or "Hug" if those words exist for him.

279 DAYS OLD | DATE:

P In general, babies with darker coloration tend to have more hair than lighter-skinned babies, who sometimes still appear to be "bald." (So hold off on your son's "Hair Club" membership for now.)

C The pronouns "I," "we," "they," and "me" are confusing for your baby because they are nonspecific. It's less confusing for her if you refer to others by their actual names.

S By ten months of age, your baby has a clearer idea of what he likes and doesn't like and may react strongly when opposed. (See below.)

Check This Out Your baby may enjoy playing with water, but when the hose is turned off or the bathtub emptied, she may protest loudly if she's not finished playing yet. If she doesn't want to be in her car seat, for instance, she may be difficult to get settled, even if the destination is someplace fun. And while she understands the word "no" and can often say it out loud, it doesn't deter her. Her willfulness is expected as part of her growing interest in independence. (Just get used to it. It's an important developmental step.)

Kids need love the most when they're acting most unloveable.

ERMA BOMBECK

280
DAYS OLD

DATE:

notes

P Fresh fruit is a better source of nutrition for your baby than fruit juice. She may have no appetite at mealtime because she is drinking too much juice.

C Ten-month-old babies usually like to play games whereby they get to investigate something interesting, like pouring Cheerios from one cup into another, or visiting a place where there are many different things to look at and touch—like a park, a museum, or a library.

S Babies about the age of yours usually enjoy music—any type—and often dance to it by bouncing, jumping, swaying, and striking a pose (to name just a few). Your baby tends to want your undivided attention and seeks your encouragement and praise.

Week 40 ends

Men are but children of a larger growth.
JOHN DRYDEN

281 DAYS OLD	DATE:	282 DAYS OLD	DATE:

Ⓟ Combining sitting with coordinated actions—such as playing with toys or turning to do something else—is a skill that is generally well established by about ten months of age.

Ⓒ Other games that appeal to this age group are the ones that make you work. The "What's that?" game makes you name every object and person in this galaxy as she points at various things. The "Dropping" game makes you retrieve whatever she drops on purpose—toys, cups, food, whatever—over and over and over. (They love this kind of stuff. Just wait till toilet training!)

Ⓢ Your baby may also enjoy people-watching at any place where large groups of people congregate. More and more, he's interested in the world outside his own.

Ⓟ By ten months of age, combining sitting with a coordinated action—such as playing with toys or turning—is a skill that may be an established part of your baby's behavior.

Ⓒ In another few weeks, your baby's use of gestures or signs to indicate her needs, observations, or questions should be fairly well established. By combining intonation, gesture, and facial expression, infants can convey both positive and negative emotions along with their message.

Ⓢ By about ten months of age, your baby may begin to attract your attention by pulling on your clothing. (If you don't want to get nabbed, wear spandex!)

Aa Bb Cc Dd Ee Ff

The hunger for love is more difficult to remove than the hunger for bread.

MOTHER TERESA

283 DAYS OLD	DATE:

284 DAYS OLD	DATE:

P By about this time (ten months of age), your baby is probably fairly skilled at rolling from his back to his stomach.

C Your baby's pincer grasp helps her pick up all the little objects parents think that they've taken care of. (No joke. There's *always* something.) However, your baby won't be able to distinguish edible from inedible substances for some time.

S You may notice that your baby is becoming temperamental at times—going from positive and helpful to negative and uncooperative in a nano-second. It's an expression of independence and it will be around for awhile (read: years).

IMPORTANT Continuous supervision will help you take a small object your baby has found away from him before he puts it into his mouth.

P By about now—around ten months of age—babies like yours can maneuver from lying face down to sitting up.

C By age ten months, your baby may begin to test the properties of an object to see how to categorize it in memory. If an infant is given a new rattle, she may inspect it, mouth it, and feel its round contours. When she shakes it and it rattles, she may shake it again and again to get the same sound. One memory category might contain "things that can be shaken and make noise" (like the rattle); another category might contain "things that feel smooth" (again, like the rattle), and so on.

S By about this time (ten to eleven months of age), your baby can begin to react to adult anger and may cry when scolded.

Some people think that as soon as you plant a tree, it must bear fruit. We must allow it to grow a bit.
TUNKU PUTRA ABDUL RAHMAN

notes

285
DAYS OLD

DATE:

Because your baby can probably voluntarily let go of something in his hand, he can offer an object to someone and actually deliver it. Your baby may not be able to deliberately throw what's in his hand until after his first birthday.

Engage in games that add words to your baby's vocabulary.

Your ten- to eleven-month-old infant may be able to imitate facial expressions. Try it out! (Be careful what faces you make because baby might be "back at ya" in a another setting.)

Did You Know? There's a more effective strategy than an angry scolding when your infant does something she shouldn't do: remove and redirect. Pick baby up and give her something interesting to do somewhere else. The added benefit is that you don't have to get angry and your baby doesn't have to get upset.

Check This Out Play this body-awareness game with your baby: Take one hand and cover your nose and say, "Where's mommy's nose?" Remove the hand and say, "Hello, nose!" Repeat for hand, elbow, and so on.

Somewhere on this globe, every ten seconds, there is a woman giving birth to a child. She must be found and stopped!

SAM LEVENSON

286 DAYS OLD	DATE:

P Take your baby for walks in her stroller to begin to train the habit of exercising (for both of you, actually).

C Between ten and eleven months of age, your baby may begin to say "mama," "dada," or some equivalent with meaning.

S Your baby is exerting his independence by wanting finger foods of his own choosing, wanting to feed himself, and wanting to pull on his own clothes. Cooperate with him when you can.

notes

287 DAYS OLD	DATE:

P Growth has slowed somewhat from the brisk pace set by the first six months partly because baby's activity burns more calories. Here are the numbers: Between ten and eleven months of age, your baby may gain about ¾ pound (340 g) in weight, ½ inch (12 mm) in length, and increase her head circumference by about ¼ inch (6 mm).

C You may enjoy playing games with your baby that improve her eye-hand coordination (see below).

S By ten to eleven months of age, your baby may want to amble under his own power, without assistance from bystanders.

Check This Out Try this: Gather easy-to-grasp toys (like blocks) and an open container (like a bucket). Show baby how to hold a block above the container and let it drop in. Can she do it? When the container fills up, baby can dump it out and try again.

Week 41 ends

A man finds out what is meant by a spitting image when he tries to feed cereal to an infant.

IMOGENE FEY

288 DAYS OLD   DATE:

289 DAYS OLD   DATE:

The small-muscle skills of a baby about the age of yours may be precise enough to help him grasp a bell by the handle or an unsharpened pencil.

Referring to a person by name represents a milestone in language development. This achievement means that your baby will begin to label other people and familiar objects and to refer to them by name. It also means she is building the type of memory system humans rely on—memories based on language.

A ten- to eleven-month-old baby may begin to assert his independence by testing his caregivers. For example, it might look like he needs help, but once a helpful caregiver arrives, he may want that person to leave so he can do it himself.

Babies about the age of yours (ten to eleven months of age) can begin to pull themselves forward with their hands.

Your baby's vocabulary of names will increase along with his vocabulary of one-syllable words like "Hi," "Bye," "What," and "No."

By ten to eleven months of age, when your baby hears you say "no-no" or call her by name in a certain tone of voice, she may restrain herself and stop what she is doing. (Time to remove and redirect?)

Love Notes Talk, sing, and read to your baby whenever you can. (It's your big chance to belt out those show tunes. They don't know how to criticize yet!)

I come from a family where gravy is considered a beverage.

ERMA BOMBECK

290	DATE:
DAYS OLD	

P Avoid shaking or spanking a baby, even playfully. The baby's head is still large and heavy relative to his body, and the severe whiplash of Shaken Baby Syndrome can result.

C Babies about the age of yours (ten to eleven months of age) may begin to look at and follow the pictures in a book while you read.

S At this age, your baby may begin to repeat actions that attract positive attention. For example, when your baby finishes a task, you might throw your arms in the air and say, "Yay!" Later baby may throw his arms into the air so you'll say "Yay" again.

291	DATE:
DAYS OLD	

P There is no known advantage in modern Western society to have infants walk early.

C Now that your baby probably understands that a hidden object still exists, she may begin to look around a corner or under a pillow for an object she saw disappear.

S Infants like yours tend to like simplicity and routine. And while they want to assert themselves more often, babies can be overwhelmed by too many choices. Two is usually a good number with an infant—a choice between one or the other of two things. Even if his choice is "both," that can work, too.

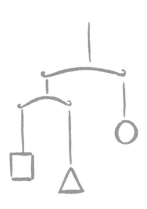

292	DATE:
DAYS OLD	

P By about ten to eleven months of age, your baby may be able to recover her balance easily while sitting.

C The gestures and signs that baby makes can reflect what he knows. For example, he might pretend to wash his hands when he sees a bar of soap.

S Control is a difficult thing for infants because their muscles are so immature. Mealtimes, using a cup, and water play are going to be messy activities, so be prepared.

Being a child is in itself a profession.
CLIFTON FADIMAN

293
DAYS OLD

DATE:

℗ Sometime between ten and eleven months of age, your baby may begin to pull herself to a sitting position. (It's one of the first events in the Iron Baby Competition.)

Ⓒ At eleven months of age, your baby is actively building his vocabulary. As you encounter and use items, name them so the associations become clear. His brain is really primed to learn right now.

Ⓢ Ten- to thirteen-month-old babies like yours actively seek the security of their caregivers, especially when frightened, tired, or ill. Make sure you are available.

294
DAYS OLD

DATE:

℗ By about ten to eleven months of age, your baby may be able to stand while holding on to furniture, but she generally sits by falling down. (It's a good thing babies' legs are short and their bottoms are padded!)

Ⓒ You'll begin to notice, if you haven't already, that your baby seems to understands much of what you say to him about himself, his play, and his habits.

Ⓢ Even though your baby is so cute and so fun at this age, don't keep her awake all day to to help her sleep at night. Babies need rest during the day, too.

Week 42 ends

Lawyers, I suppose, were children once.
CHARLES LAMB

295 DAYS OLD	DATE:

296 DAYS OLD	DATE:

P Now that your baby is ten months old, he may be able to make coordinated, alternating stepping movements. (He may or may not be holding on to your hands for support.)

C Repetition and rephrasing help your baby learn language. Repetition gives baby more exposure to words so they become familiar, and rephrasing lets her know that there are many ways to express an idea.

S Now that your baby knows that you are a special person, his goal seems to be to stay physically close to you as well. Now that he's mobile, it's easier for him to do just that. (He wants to be your little shadow.)

Check This Out Narrating baby's experiences is an easy way to help her learn the language. For example, you might say, "Are you ready? Let's go . . . okay? Let's go . . . here we are outside." What seems slow and redundant to you won't seem so to your baby.

P Between ten and eleven months of age, your baby may offer a toy to another person, but may not release it even though he can voluntarily let go of something in his grasp.

C Babies learn at their own pace. Don't pressure your baby to learn a new skill when she resists; don't force baby to perform a learned skill when she pushes back. Some days she may feel more like performing; sometimes her brain or body isn't ready for the next step.

S Take into account what you know of your baby's personality or temperament if you anticipate change. If at all possible, make the transition gradually.

There is no cure for birth and death save to enjoy the interval.

GEORGE SANTAYANA

297 DAYS OLD	DATE:	298 DAYS OLD	DATE:

P By the time he's eleven months old—in a few week's time—your baby should be fairly skilled at getting around by crawling, creeping, scooting, rolling, pushing, hitching, and pulling (or any other way they get around).

C Chances are, you've already begun to modify your speech when talking to your baby. Use short sentences, a simplified vocabulary, attention-getting expressions such as "Look!" and exaggerated pronunciation to provide a clear model of the language.

S Your baby's need for closeness might set up an interesting push-pull dynamic. If baby's additional demands for comfort and closeness make you feel impatient or irritable, your baby may sense these negative emotions and feel less secure as a result. This development might lead your baby to demand *even more* lap time and reassurance, not less, during this phase. Indulge your child and yourself. It's the easiest way to get back on track.

Check This Out What kinds of events are stressful to infants? Even positive experiences like moving and meeting family members for the first time are stressful because they involve change. You and your baby have to adapt to the new circumstances together.

Love Notes The more the caregiver pushes away the baby who wants extra closeness, the stronger the baby's need to be close to the caregiver becomes. Remember to continue to show your baby physical affection as she gets older.

P Babies about eleven months of age generally need at least one good nap per day. (Ah, sweet sleep.)

C Another way to help your child learn language is to describe what your baby is doing or is about to do. For example, "You're reading a book. Good!" or "That's right. Pick up your bear."

S The type and quantity of toys available to your baby are far less important than all the ways you have of showing and telling your baby that you love her and feel attached to her.

notes

We are born naked, wet, and hungry. Then things get worse.

ANONYMOUS

(P) Making stepping movements with feet on a flat surface is generally well established by now—ten to eleven months of age.

(C) Encourage your child to use speech or speech and gesture combined to communicate. While it is easier to point or whine, the more your baby is able to practice forming sounds into words, the more language-proficient he may become.

(S) Just as your baby wants your attention and closeness more, she is equally adamant about wanting much less contact between herself and someone unfamiliar. (You've become a push-and-pull toy!)

Love Notes Accept any effort by your baby to communicate first, even if the sound is just a noise or a breath. Praise him warmly. Then sometimes ask for a little bit more, and praise him for anything that comes close. Take small steps, expect plateaus and negative progress, and give him genuine affection for his hard work.

(P) Even if your ten- to eleven-month-old can take a few steps, he may still drop down on all fours and revert to crawling for speed and efficiency. (It's the baby version of four-wheel drive.)

(C) Your baby is going to learn to imitate the language she hears spoken around her. If she hears baby talk, slang, disrespectful speech, or cussing, she will incorporate those words into her speech.

(S) Your time and attention will always be the most powerful rewards you have to offer your baby at ten months of age or ten years.

It's not how much we give, but how much love we put into giving.

MOTHER TERESA

notes

301
DAYS OLD

DATE:

While your baby has probably seen someone demonstrate how to scribble, your baby may not attempt to put crayon to paper until he is at least eleven months old.

As young language learners, babies produce facsimiles of correct speech. Respond to your baby's statements by clarifying—"Oh, you want down? Okay."—and elaborating—"Bite? Bite of fruit? A banana?" then show her the banana.

Babies who feel safe and protected have more energy to try out new skills. This is true for boy and girl babies alike.

Did You Know? The most competent babies have loving and reliable caregivers.

Week 43 ends

If you have much, give of your wealth; if you have little, give of your heart.
ARAB PROVERB

Week 44 Begins

302 DAYS OLD   DATE:

303 DAYS OLD   DATE:

P The incisors on each side of the two lower teeth may begin to appear by about eleven months of age.

C Have conversations with your baby in which you play the role of both speaker and listener. She will hear spoken language along with the inflection used to communicate, and she'll come to understand the elements of pacing and turn-taking.

S By about eleven months of age, your baby may begin to spill food or pull hard on an object, for example, because of an interest in what will follow his action. This behavior may also be an invitation for interaction.

P By about this time (eleven months of age) your baby may demonstrate a clear preference for some foods over others. She might reject foods she loved when she was younger and embrace something new and different at mealtime.

C Start to describe the shape, color, size, and location of items. You can use comparative terms like "round" and "square," "blue" and "red," "big" and "little," and "in" and "out," for example.

S Position yourself to maximize eye-to-eye contact with your baby. Such eye contact conveys interest and is a good way to get his attention (and to get another look at his cute face).

304 DAYS OLD   DATE:

P By the time your baby is around eleven months of age, his fine motor skills may help him deliberately place small objects and remove them from a tight-fitting enclosure. (Well done, pincer grasp!)

C Use polite words—such as *please* and *thank you*—around your baby if you want those words included in her vocabulary.

S Your eleven-month-old baby may react to restrictions with frustration. She wants her way and doesn't have the brain power to be patient, because the emotional center of her brain is more well developed than the rational center.

If there is anything we wish to change in the child, we should first examine it and see
whether it is not something that could be better changed in ourselves.

CARL JUNG

notes

305
DAYS OLD

DATE:

By about now—at ten months of age—your baby may be able to move from sitting down to a creeping position. To be able to move forward while balancing his own weight on his arms and legs represents an important advance in large-muscle skill.

Respond to your baby's vocalizations or gestures by elaborating the response. If your baby indicates she wants "up," you might respond by saying, "Do you want up? Okay, up we go!" for instance. In this case, your baby gets to hear language, see the behavior demonstrated, and interact with you all at once. Clever baby!

Continue to respond to your infant's distress in a timely fashion. Maintain the confidence your baby has in you to take care of his needs as quickly and efficiently as possible.

306
DAYS OLD

DATE:

By the time your baby is eleven months old, she may be able to pivot to reach backward to pick up an object while seated.

If you have inverted a plastic mug to cover a toy, by eleven months of age, your baby may be able to grasp the handle with one hand and lift it as part of a well-coordinated skill.

Give your baby unconditional love. Unconditional love has no strings attached—it never depends on anything your baby does or says, and it can never be lost or suspended. It's love that sustains itself.

The meaning of life is to give life meaning.
ANONYMOUS

3 0 7 DAYS OLD	DATE:

P By about eleven months of age, your baby may walk either while holding on to furniture or with both hands held.

C By now your baby may be fairly proficient at jabbering. Even though the sounds are actually double-takes. For example, you might find yourself asking your baby, "What did I hear you say?" or asking your partner, "Did he say what I think he said?"

S You probably have noticed that your baby engages in both solitary play (alone and by herself) and interactive play (with a partner). When baby interacts, actual games can be played, such as peek-a-boo, patty-cake, the eensy-weensy spider, "I'm going to get you/tickle you," and "sooo big."

Love Notes Loving unconditionally is the most secure and valuable love you can offer another person. And poignantly, it's the love that we yearn for ourselves.

3 0 8 DAYS OLD	DATE:

P If your baby is having trouble staying asleep once he is put to bed, go to baby's bedside to quiet him after he wakes up. If you pick him up, feed him, or take him to bed with you, he may wake up on other occasions and expect the same type of treatment. Thus, a baby who has been able to sleep through the night can be retrained to awaken if some type of interesting attention awaits him.

C By about eleven months of age, your baby may be able to engage in sequential play. An example of this type of play is when your baby stacks rings on a spool one after the other.

S Just as your baby wants time close to you, she also needs time apart. Make appropriate adjustments in baby's planned activities to allow for some free play in a supervised environment.

Week 44 ends

notes

_____

_____

_____

_____

_____

_____

_____

_____

Keep your face to the sunshine and you can never see the shadow.

HELEN KELLER

DATE:

309 DAYS OLD

DATE:

310 DAYS OLD

P At some point, your baby may begin to take some steps without support. When he can walk three steps without holding on, he's right on the cusp of walking alone. ("And they're off! Rounding the first turn is Your Baby, a new entry, followed by the pack.")

C The typical ten- to eleven-month-old baby has an attention span of about three or four minutes. Babies this age tend to prefer rhymes to narrative stories because of their tempo and interesting sounds.

S Consistency and mutual support are key elements of parenting. Ideally, all of the caregivers in your baby's life keep the lines of communication open, have a "game plan" to use as a guide, and can count on each other's support.

Did You Know? The timeframe for normal walking extends all the way through month sixteen.

Check This Out How can you keep your baby focused a little longer on a story? Try stopping from time to time to point out or describe what she sees on the page. For example, "Wow! Look at that. There's a boy and a dog and a cow."

P Your baby's ability to use his thumb and forefinger with precision when reaching and grasping is generally well established by now—about eleven months of age.

C Learning to identify items as "same" and "different" is an important skill. When a one-year-old baby is given a set of four trees and four people, for example, she may be able to select all four of one kind about 40 percent of the time.

S Parents set up boundaries to keep infants safe and establish respect for other people and their property. Parents enforce these boundaries by reminders and disciplinary actions. During infancy, that usually means that the child is reminded to stop, is moved from the area, or has to exchange the item for an appropriate one.

We all live under the same sky, but we don't have the same horizon.

KONRAD ADENAUER

3 1 1 DAYS OLD	DATE:

P Try to make the environment as safe as you can for your baby to explore. Even then, protect your baby with constant supervision, since he is absolutely fearless at this age.

C When you listen to your baby vocalize, what sounds do you hear? Circle the ones in this list, and add others if you need to: "ay," "ah," "aan," "da," "eh," "erg," "goo," "la," "ma," "mu."
Others:_____

_____.

S If the TV is off-limits, for example, remind baby when she approaches, "No, no. Don't touch." If baby touches, parents should probably relocate her and give her something interesting to do. (There are lots of trips like this. It comes with the territory!)

3 1 2 DAYS OLD	DATE:

P By about eleven months of age, your baby may be able to walk by inching along sideways while hanging on to a planter or furniture with both hands.

C Listen for baby's repeated syllable sounds when she is vocalizing (e.g., "da-da," "nah-nah"). She may be able to produce four different repeated syllable pairs by the time she is twelve to thirteen months old.

S Infant self-control develops as the responsibility for enforcing limits shifts from the parents to the child himself. The ultimate goal is for baby to remember where the boundaries are and keep himself out of trouble.

The great gift of family life is to be intimately acquainted with people you might never even introduce yourself to, had life not done it for you.
KENDALL HAILEY

313 DAYS OLD DATE:

314 DAYS OLD DATE:

In another month or so your baby may be able to walk while holding on with only one hand and not two.

Keep listening for more variation in your baby's vocalizations. By about now, babies can begin to produce variation in the syllables they babble, combining different sounds on repetition, like "ba-bi-ba-bi" or "da-bi-da-bi." Jot down any you hear your baby use:

_____

_____

_____

_____ .

When a ten-month-old baby like yours is playing with a parent and a stranger enters the room, the securely attached baby will use the attached parent as a physical touch-back point and a visual reference.

Check This Out You may begin to notice that your baby's babbles are beginning to sound like actual words, because the syllables have well-formed consonant-vowel sequences in them.

By about this time, your baby can usually eat what the rest of the family does as long as it is chopped, smashed, or blended into small pieces.

Near the end of baby's first year, she may be able to understand a few short sentences, not because she understands the verbal language as such but because of body language and cues such as "Want up?" "Open," "Take a bite," and "Let me see your hands."

One of the first responses your baby had to his mirror image was to smile. Smiling at his reflection in the mirror may be well established by now.

notes

_____

_____

_____

_____

_____

_____

_____

_____

_____

_____

_____

_____

_____

Where we love is home—home that our feet may leave, but not our hearts.

OLIVER WENDELL HOLMES

3 1 5
DAYS OLD

DATE:

P Offer your baby three small meals a day plus two or three nutritious snacks to meet her energy and growth needs. (Have a few yourself!)

C Chances are your baby will be fairly consistent about responding to his own name by his first birthday.

S Your baby may become much more animated when playing with her own image in the mirror. She may laugh, pat, bang, reach for, lean toward, or "mouth" the baby in the mirror.

IMPORTANT Avoid hot dog pieces, raisins, peanut butter, whole grapes, cherries with pits, hard candies, or other foods that may be hard to chew or could cause choking.

Week 45 ends

Nowadays we want our children to make their own decisions, but we expect those decisions to please us.
BRUNO BETTELHEIM

Week 46 Begins

Ⓟ Compared to older children, infants are more likely to develop infections of their ears and lungs because their systems are immature and trap bacteria easily. Watch their behavior for signs of discomfort.

Ⓒ By about twelve months of age, your baby may respond to the telephone ringing by looking at you or looking at the phone. He may anticipate you talking on the phone. He may also start to clamor for your attention, since he knows you will focus on the call and not on him.

Ⓢ Waving "bye-bye" is a skill that may be well established by your baby's first birthday. (International babies wave "Ciao!")

Ⓟ Fat is essential for the proper development of your baby's brain and nervous system. Infants don't need low-fat or fat-free diets.

Ⓒ Your baby's ability to uncover a hidden toy is usually well established by about now—at twelve months old.

Ⓢ Most likely, your eleven- to twelve-month-old baby can participate in active cooperative play.

Check This Out Play this game with your baby: Initiate a game of peek-a-boo by hiding your face behind a mirror or a piece of paper and then reappearing from different sides of it. If your baby tried to look around first one and then another edge of the paper, she's playing actively and cooperatively.

Praise is like champagne; it should be served while it is still bubbling.

ROBBINS READER

318 DAYS OLD DATE:

319 DAYS OLD DATE:

If you haven't already, start to brush your baby's teeth, gums, and tongue. Use a soft-bristled wet toothbrush (no paste yet) and make small, circular jiggling motions at an angle to the gums.

Within the next month or so, your baby may be able to use selective hearing to ignore background noise or focus her attention sharply on the sounds she wants to listen to.

Even by your baby's first birthday, he is still learning to feed himself by using fingers, spoon, and cup (with much spilling). He can usually help with dressing, though, by putting a foot out for a shoe or pushing an arm through a sleeve.

Both baby boys and baby girls may take their first steps on tiptoe. Why? Because the toes touch down first, the stepping reflex may propel the body forward. Using the sole of the entire foot to take a step is a skill your baby needs to practice.

By eleven or twelve months of age, your baby might not only respond to his caregiver's departure but also anticipate her leaving. Anticipation is cued by the repeated behaviors that are part of the ritual of preparing to leave (e.g., pick up the car keys, grab the lunch sack, et cetera).

From about eleven months onward, your baby may take a liking to the attention that performing for an audience brings. She is thoroughly cute and uninhibited now. Saturate your memory with her delightful performances!

If a child lives with approval, he learns to like himself.
DOROTHY LAW NOLTE

notes

320
DAYS OLD

DATE:

Your baby will probably be quite proficient at imitating simple actions by his first birthday. For example, if he watches you poke a finger into an empty hole in a pegboard or put a block into a cup, describe your actions and then invite baby to replicate the action—he usually can.

As your baby learns her native language, she may temporarily stop using some of her first words as she learns new words. No worries. She'll reincorporate those words into her vocabulary shortly.

The development of a secure attachment between caregivers and the newborn is essential, because it keeps the baby close and motivates adults to provide care. Attachment continues to be a lifeline for basic survival, but it also keeps your baby alive and emotionally healthy.

Any kid who has two parents who are interested in him and a houseful of books isn't poor.

SAM LEVENSON

3 2 1	DATE:
DAYS OLD	

ℙ Babies as old as yours (eleven to twelve months of age) are usually coordinated enough to bring their hands together at the midlines of bodies, particularly when they have a toy in one or both hands.

ℂ Now that your baby is about eleven months old, she may not only understand the meaning of "no," but she might repeat the word and shake her head as well. (This often occurs while she continues to walk toward something she can't have!)

𝒮 At six months, if your baby was more sedate and played alone quietly with his toys, at twelve months he'll also be sedate and go to sleep easily and eat slowly, for example. ("Laid back," we might say.)

Love Notes Securely attached babies have caregivers who are cooperative, accessible, sensitive, and accepting. The acronym is "CASA" (like the Spanish word for home). Consciously cultivate these attributes. If you lapse, renew yourself.

3 2 2	DATE:
DAYS OLD	

ℙ As your baby gets more practiced at walking, you'll notice that the steps become more sure and the foot placement more precise. Do you know what babies do next? They *run*! (You'll have to, too, of course.)

ℂ Now that your baby is eleven months old, he may be able to follow simple directions such as "Come here." It's not long before he knows so well what "Come here" means that he'll bolt in the opposite direction. (Time to try "Go away" in order to get a rebound effect?) Just enjoy the word games he plays.

𝒮 Promote a secure attachment in your infant by promptly identifying and attending to his needs.

Week 46 ends

notes

_____
_____
_____
_____
_____
_____
_____
_____
_____
_____
_____

Not all those who wander are lost.

J. R. R. TOLKIEN

Week 47 Begins

323 DAYS OLD DATE:

324 DAYS OLD DATE:

Ⓟ Almost all eleven-month-old babies like yours are bowlegged. Supported by nutrition that builds healthy bones, walking practice tends to push baby's knees together and moves her ankles apart.

Ⓒ Since your baby is sensitive to cues that signal you're about to leave, follow a departure routine that might include hugs, kisses, smiles, hand waves, and the promise of returning, and use it each time you go out. If you help your baby distinguish between your leaving the house and your leaving his field of vision, he may understand your behavior better.

Ⓢ At six months, if your baby was more predictable and woke up and ate at about the same times each day, at twelve months she'll also be predictable and have regular bowel movements, for example.

Did You Know? The alignment of baby's knees and ankles isn't generally a problem unless the developmental pattern of one leg is different from the other.

Ⓟ Serious injury from falls is uncommon provided your baby has no access to hazardous areas (like stairs) and is fully supervised.

Ⓒ Accustom your baby to several sitters so that you always have familiar people to call upon.

Ⓢ At six months, if your baby was cooperative and quieted if you gave her a toy, or talked or sang to her, at twelve months of age she'll also be cooperative and allow parents to soothe her, for example.

Nothing you do for children is ever wasted. They seem not to notice us, hovering, averting our eyes, and they seldom offer thanks, but what we do for them is never wasted.

GARRISON KEILLOR

325 DAYS OLD	DATE:

326 DAYS OLD	DATE:

Ⓟ Throughout infancy, the same factors continue to be important in helping baby make developmental progress—excellent nutrition, sufficient sleep, good health, a safe environment, a secure emotional attachment anchored by tons of love, and the ability to practice the skills he needs to master.

Ⓒ While your baby is now probably using gestures and cues to interpret your verbal messages, she may use signs, gestures, and other codes to communicate with you. For example, if you are warning her to stay away from the hot oven door, your baby may respond by saying, "No! No!" to indicate she understands the prohibition (or at least *heard* it).

Ⓢ One way that caregivers promote secure attachment in their infants is to take the inevitable problems and limitations imposed on them as parents in stride.

Ⓟ Climbing up stairs is a skill your baby should be allowed to practice but only when you are there to take each step with him.

Ⓒ Select toys you think your baby will enjoy without worrying too much about their color or whether they are for boys or girls. Your baby will better understand who he is by the way you refer to him. For example, you might say, "You are my best baby boy, yes you are!"

Ⓢ Before you leave your infant with a new caregiver, give everyone a chance to get acquainted, talk, and play in the setting where your baby will stay.

notes

_____
_____
_____
_____
_____
_____
_____
_____
_____
_____
_____

If you give your son only one gift, let it be enthusiasm.

BRUCE BARTON

DATE:

DATE:

P Even though most families watch some television, you'll want to limit the amount of time your baby watches so his day can include activities that will help keep him physically fit.

C If your usual babysitter is unavailable and you need someone to come and stay with your baby, don't assume that a caregiver with similar characteristics won't be exposed as an imposter. Remember (you, too!) that your baby's memory is improving daily.

S At six months, if your baby was more wary about new places and people, at twelve months she may also be wary and stay somber and stiff when she's picked up by friendly but less familiar people, for example.

Did You Know? For most babies, learning to walk downstairs is more difficult than walking up.

P Attachment may be facilitated by the way babies are carried by their mothers. Compared to mothers who carried their babies in plastic infant seats, mothers who used slings or fabric carriers to "wear" their children and had close physical contact were twice as likely to be securely attached to their babies.

C Your baby may be particularly attentive to familiar words, such as "baby," "mama," and "up" for example. He might indicate recognition by changing his facial expression, vocalizing, or by trying to imitate the word.

S All infants need accessible caregivers who will prioritize their baby's needs. "Accessible" means there and responsive, not just physically present.

One of the most obvious facts about grownups to a child is that they have forgotten what it is like to be a child.

RANDALL JARRELL

329 DATE:
DAYS OLD

(P) Depending on the time of year, your baby might come down with a cold. Work toward prevention by consistently washing baby's hands or using hand sanitizer after playing or arriving home and before eating no matter what the season. (That goes for everybody.)

(C) If your baby is given a bell or a rattle, she may shake it just to hear the noise. The understanding that certain actions paired with certain objects have predictable outcomes is an expectation based on previous experience. Your baby will be fairly skilled at remembering what leads to what by thirteen months of age.

(S) If your baby adjusted relatively easily to change at six months of age and disliked new faces at first but then accepted them, she'll also be adaptable at twelve months, fearing toy animals at first, but then enjoying them, for example.

IMPORTANT If your baby is choking, don't put your fingers into the baby's mouth to remove an object unless you can see it and easily grasp it. Otherwise, you risk pushing the object farther down his throat. If you can't easily remove the object, call 9-1-1 for advice.

Week 47 ends

I hear in the chamber above me the patter of little feet, the sound of a door that is opened and voices soft and sweet.

HENRY WADSWORTH LONGFELLOW

Week 48 Begins

DATE:

330
DAYS OLD

DATE:

331
DAYS OLD

The American Dental Association recommends that your baby visit a pediatric dentist by her first birthday.

You may have noticed your eleven-month-old baby beginning to look at one or more pictures in a familiar book with interest or recognition. Open one of these books with him and say, "Look!" in an interested manner and watch what he does.

By the end of baby's first year, she may still cry for attention and out of frustration and fear, especially around unfamiliar people.

In another year—around age two—your baby's brain may go from weighing 50 percent of an adult's brain to 75 percent of that weight. (That's like investing $100 and, in a year, getting $150 in return!)

Infants like routine and predictability because they'll know what's coming next. As a consequence, they can relax and cooperate. Try to establish as many routines as you can (e.g., bedtime, bath time, and so on). You might be bored, but your baby will love it!

Babies who are securely attached frequently look at, smile at, stay close to, follow, and give objects to their caregivers.

Did You Know? Why do infants cry? Early on, crying is for the essentials—hunger, fatigue, and discomfort. Later on, cries can reflect disappointment, frustration, loneliness, and fear.

The greatest oak was once a little nut who held its ground.
UNKNOWN

332
DAYS OLD

DATE:

notes

P Between eleven and twelve months of age, baby's distance vision may improve from sitting at 20 inches (51 cm) to see what most adults can see at a distance of 200 inches (16.7 feet, or 5 m), to sitting at 20 inches (51 cm) to see what most adults would see at a distance of 40 to 60 inches (3.3 to 5 feet, or 1 to 1.5 m).

C First words may appear as early as eight months or as late as fourteen months. Most babies can say at least one word by their first birth-day. (Credit card? No, that's two words.)

S The nature and quality of baby's social game-playing may change noticeably by about twelve months of age. Babies in object-exchange games take turns regularly and confidently. Later they may invent or play new games with their caregivers.

We could never have loved the earth so well if we had had no childhood on it.
GEORGE ELIOT

333 DAYS OLD   DATE:

334 DAYS OLD   DATE:

Ⓟ Children between one and two years of age run a higher risk of choking than any other age group because they are skilled at picking things up and putting them into their mouths. In addition, they can't yet remember the difference between what's edible and what's dangerous.

Ⓒ Babies who use sign language and babies who speak follow roughly the same developmental timetable of language acquisition. By about thirteen months, hard-of-hearing babies have learned about ten signs. And just like hearing infants, they'll start to combine signs, like "baby up," into short sentences by around seventeen months.

Ⓢ In about another month or so, your baby's ability to perform actions that she has never seen before in order to solve problems should be fairly well established.

IMPORTANT If your baby can cough, breathe, or cry, he isn't choking.

Ⓟ Lowering oneself from a standing to a sitting position on the floor requires muscle control and balance. Baby may use a handrail or a piece of furniture, but sitting from a standing position is generally well established by about this time—eleven months of age.

Ⓒ The length of time your baby spends in focused attention will be longer if only one toy is presented rather than several.

Ⓢ By this time (eleven months of age), you may notice your baby deliberately trying to communicate messages to you or others. For example, your baby might attract your attention and try to convey that he wants "up" or he is looking for the dog.

For an artist nothing is ever lacking, no places empty of resources. Even in a prison with soundproof walls a royal treasure of childhood memories enriches your solitude.

RAINER MARIA RILKE

335 DAYS OLD	DATE:

336 DAYS OLD	DATE:

P Your baby's body is working at replacing the cartilage in the soft spot on top of the skull with bone. The soft spot might be almost closed by her first birthday. (The correct question is: What is the anterior fontanel?)

C Deferred imitation—imitation that occurs hours or days after it was seen—is increasingly common after your baby's first birthday. For example, one baby might watch another baby have a tantrum but not have one that resembles it until hours or days later.

S The only signal your newborn had to cue you was to cry. Now, at about eleven months of age, your baby may begin to attract your attention by calling you by name.

Did You Know? Attention span is critical to being able to concentrate and learn. The longer baby's attention span is, the better.

P Some babies are more interested in making marks on paper than others. When supplied with paper and a crayon, your baby may begin to scribble spontaneously sometime between now (eleven months of age) and sixteen months of age.

C By about twelve months, and maybe earlier, babies may begin to understand that some objects and living things are abstract—that is, not part of their immediate experience. For example, the characteristics of tigers, submarines, and tropical flowers can become familiar and eventually understood, even without being actively encountered.

S By one year of age, your baby might be able to convey that she feels sad, angry, afraid, disgusted, happy, and surprised. (What do you suppose would disgust a baby? Grandpa in a Speedo? Grandma in a thong?)

Week 48 ends

notes

A family is a unit composed not only of children, but of men, women,
and an occasional animal, and the common cold.

OGDEN NASH

337 DAYS OLD   DATE:

338 DAYS OLD   DATE:

P Sometime between now and sixteen months of age, your baby will be able to deliberately throw something in his grasp for the sake of throwing. Prior to this development, he could let go of something voluntarily but could not propel it. (Expect things to come flying from everywhere. Baby has no sense of direction.)

C Babies learn through investigation and exploration, and they adapt to new situations more readily if those explorations have been varied and diverse.

S By the time your baby is twelve months of age, she might display the emotion of affection by giving a kiss or a hug.

P If people in baby's family are allergic to certain foods (such as peanuts, cow's milk, wheat, and so on), check with your baby's health-care provider about introducing them into your baby's diet.

C By your baby's first birthday, he knows the meaning of several words—usually the names of pets, family members, familiar objects (his bottle or blanket), and the word "No." More significantly, your baby may be able to use two or three words with meaning in the correct context. For example, if mother says, "Let the dog come in," and baby says the word for dog, then he's indicating that he understands what's going on.

S Your baby is still happiest in familiar surroundings. (No trips to exotic places just yet.)

"Funnyface / Or elephant as yet / Mean nothing."
W. H. AUDEN

339 DAYS OLD	DATE:

By about twelve months of age, your baby may be able to walk holding on to a piece of furniture with one hand.

Your baby's first words are simple and within her experience, but they may not be "mama" or "dada," so brace yourself. (Make that a double brace, especially if you get beat out by the dog!)

Your baby will learn a lot by watching the way you interact with others. Since your style could easily become her style, make sure you're proud of what you're doing and saying in her presence.

Did You Know? The ability to use words meaningfully in the appropriate context is a milestone achievement for your baby. It lays the foundation for all future word acquisition and communication skills.

340 DAYS OLD	DATE:

All areas of development don't necessarily keep pace with one another. Instead, your baby's physical, cognitive, and social-emotional skills seem to develop in phases. For example, one child might be an earlier talker but a later walker; another child might want to be the center of everyone's attention but also like books and blocks. It's hard to predict what your baby's pattern will be.

Around your baby's first birthday, she may begin to recognize objects by name. For example, you might ask "Where's the cup?" and baby might pick a cup up from her tray.

If your baby is clinging tightly to you, he is probably afraid. Draw him in close and give him reassurance. When he's more comfortable, his grip will relax.

Growing up and growing old are a continuous process of learning what one cannot do well.
EVELYN WAUGH

34 1 DAYS OLD	DATE:

℗ By eleven months of age or so, your baby may attempt to walk backward. Walking backward is a complex skill that might take six to eight months more to establish.

Ⓒ You may notice that by the time your baby is about a year old, he may imitate animal sounds. Usually, they're common, garden-variety animals (not the collared peccary or the capybara).

Ⓢ Because your baby has gotten really good at identifying who is familiar and who is not, her world can seem a lot scarier. Factor this height-ened awareness of strangers in with the discomfort she feels around them, and add the idea that you might not be accessible, and all of that can make a comfort object look really good to her right now. You may notice more of an attachment or a new attachment to a blanket or toy. It's harmless and provides portable comfort. (Sounds good—cheaper than therapy!)

Check This Out Play this game with your baby: Dem-onstrate walking backward by pulling a toy. Now hand the pull-toy's string to your baby and encourage him to pull the toy along the floor.

34 2 DAYS OLD	DATE:

℗ There are lots of stimulating toys and games available for infants. However, if the pace of the toy or game is too fast, or she's not motivated to acquire the skills that might interest you, back off for now. There's lots of time.

Ⓒ Babies can function more easily if they are able to be calmed or can calm themselves down. This can avoid excessively irritable, clinging, hyper, or panicked behavior.

Ⓢ Prioritize your baby's needs and balance their wants.

notes

_____

_____

_____

_____

_____

_____

_____

_____

_____

_____

_____

_____

_____

Childhood is something so close, so special . . . It's something you ought to keep to yourself. The way you keep back tears.

FRANÇOISE GIROUD

343
DAYS OLD

DATE:

notes

Ⓟ Accidents and big messes are going to happen during infancy because your baby is still so new at coordinating his muscles, senses, and thinking. Have realistic expectations about your child's ability . . . and have realistic expectations about yourself as well.

Ⓒ Bribing baby to eat food in order to get a reward is not recommended. Western culture has all kinds of food issues, not the least of which is childhood obesity. Your baby should eat because he's hungry.

Ⓢ If your baby adjusted relatively easily to change at six months of age and disliked new environments at first but then accepted them, she'll also be adaptable at twelve months, at first displaying uncertainty about new play settings, for example, but then enjoying them.

Check This Out Encourage your baby to pass developmental milestones and keep track of her progress, but don't push her to be your idea of a "Superbaby." That goal might frustrate both of you.

Week 49 ends

Babies are always more trouble than you thought—and more wonderful.
CHARLES OSGOOD

Week 50 Begins

344
DAYS OLD

DATE:

345
DAYS OLD

DATE:

By your baby's first birthday, he may begin to put one block on top of another to build a tower. This activity is great eye-hand coordination practice.

The visual system of the twelve-month-old baby is generally able to track rapidly moving objects such as cars in traffic, the movement of objects and people on TV, and fast-moving people and animals.

In general, babies seem designed to take an interest in sights, sounds, and people. That tendency helps them fit into their families and communities better.

Your one-year-old baby usually has sufficient eye-hand coordination to be able to pick up a block on her own and release it into a container if she has seen you do just that.

By about twelve months of age, your baby may be able to control and adjust his response to a sound. He can decide if he wants to listen to it or ignore it and what kind of a reaction the sound warrants.

It's easier for baby to function well if she's not excessively withdrawn or shy.

Children are the anchors that hold a mother to life.
SOPHOCLES

346 DAYS OLD   DATE:

347 DAYS OLD   DATE:

By the time your baby is about twelve months of age, your baby can probably turn the pages of a book more smoothly and efficiently than when she was younger.

By about twelve months of age, your baby may be able to use selective hearing to ignore a sound when she first hears it. (Her parents may do just that with the first ring of their alarm clock on a work day!)

In general, babies seem designed to focus their attention and not be excessively distractible. That tendency helps them fit into their families and communities better.

Babies who are around twelve months of age are typically very active. They seem determined to practice getting around their world.

After baby has mastered a skill like waving bye-bye, he may not wave every time he's asked. It's not that your baby has forgotten how to wave; instead, he may be single-mindedly focused on something else or temporarily bored with "bye-bye."

Babies also seem to be designed to enjoy a variety of different sounds and different rhythms. That's good because ours is an acoustic world.

notes

Having children makes you no more a parent than having a piano makes you a pianist.
MICHAEL LEVINE

348 DAYS OLD   DATE:

349 DAYS OLD   DATE:

P Although the number of naps per day varies, napping continues to be essential to your baby's brain development, learning, and memory. Sleep also decreases the level of a hormone associated with stress, thereby helping your baby manage stress better. (This goes for adults, too. Ahh, even sweeter sleep.)

C By about twelve months of age, your baby may search for an object *even if she hasn't seen it hidden*, looking where the object was last seen. This behavior represents a cognitive milestone for your baby. The more persistence she displays in searching for a disappeared or hidden item, the more convinced she seems to be of its continued existence.

S In general, babies seem designed to tolerate being changed, dressed, and bathed. That tendency helps them fit into their families and communities better.

P By about twelve months of age, your baby's head and chest circumference are about equal. (If that was true of adults, too, we'd all look like dumbbells.)

C By about twelve months of age, babies can begin to tell the difference between simple geometric forms like a circle and a triangle. (Wow. Geometry starts in infancy. Who knew?)

S It might seem like worries about strangers coming and parents leaving emotionally hobble the one-year-old. Actually, they are signs of a strong and healthy caregiver-child attachment. When a child doesn't have this emotional bond, even a caregiver can seem like a stranger or a stranger can seem like a potential caregiver.

The more people have studied different methods of bringing up children, the more they have come to the conclusion that what good mothers and fathers instinctively feel like doing for their babies is the best after all.

BENJAMIN SPOCK

350
DAYS OLD

DATE:

notes

(P) In general, babies seem designed to enjoy being held and moved up and down and from side to side. That tendency helps them fit into their families and communities better.

(C) Your baby's ability to repeat two syllables of the same sound, such as "ba-ba" or "ma-ma" is usually well established by his first birthday. (This form of repetition is called *babbling*.)

(S) Visually, infants seem to enjoy a variety of things to look at, including reasonably bright lights, visual designs, facial expressions, and moving objects.

Week 50 ends

A baby changes your dinner party conversation from politics to poop.

MAURICE JOHNSTONE

3 5 1
DAYS OLD

DATE:

3 5 2
DAYS OLD

DATE:

(P) Between eleven and twelve months of age, you can expect your baby to gain about ¾ pound (340 g) in weight, to grow about ½ inch (1.27 cm) in length, and to increase his head circumference by about ¼ inch (0.6 cm).

(C) Your baby probably won't have 20/20 vision until she is four or five years old.

(S) In general, babies are more comfortable around strangers who approach them gradually and quietly than strangers who are loud, sudden, and approach too closely.

(P) By your baby's first birthday, he could have as many as six to eight baby teeth, all sharp and useful. (Mostly sharp.)

(C) By the time your baby is a year old, she will understand that even if she doesn't see the contents of a box, if she can hear something in the box make noise, there's something in the box.

(S) One of the most dynamic forces experienced during infancy is the strong pull toward the attachment figures in his life and the strong push away from anyone unfamiliar. The tension is especially high during this time in your child's life—seven to twelve months of age.

As new working parents, we all go from being couples who finish each other's sentences to being people who never even heard the first half of the sentence.

LOUISE LAGUE

353 DAYS OLD DATE:

354 DAYS OLD DATE:

P One developmental accomplishment of the first twelve months is climbing. Climbing is used in social interaction (climbing into someone's lap) and problem solving (climbing to retrieve a toy baby wants).

C Your baby's ability to acquire solutions to problems through imitation usually requires him to imitate actions he can't see himself doing, like pursing his lips to blow out.

S In general, your baby will be more comfortable in the presence of a stranger who is younger, female, and smaller (and who is kneeling and sitting rather than standing) than a stranger who is older, male, and larger in size.

Check This Out How to handle the separation and stranger concerns? The best advice may be the course you've already been following—give baby the warm, responsive protection that she asks for around strangers, and only leave your baby with people to whom she is well attached.

Did You Know? Like creeping or crawling, climbing helps acquaint your baby with her three-dimensional world.

P Now that your baby is eleven months old he may begin to move from standing to squatting or squatting to standing without losing his balance. (Squatting is also an event in the Iron Baby Competition.)

C Now, at almost twelve months of age, your baby is increasing her efforts to control the amount of attention she directs toward a task. Even though the ability to concentrate, retain focus, and avoid distraction takes years to perfect, your baby may show a major increase in her attention span and focused level of interest in the next half year, by eighteen months of age. (And not a moment too soon!)

S In general, your baby will be more comfortable with a stranger who comes to the house than a stranger who is encountered in public.

notes

_____
_____
_____
_____
_____
_____
_____
_____
_____
_____
_____

I guess the real reason that my wife and I had children is the same reason that Napoleon had for invading Russia: it seemed like a good idea at the time.

BILL COSBY

355 DAYS OLD

DATE:

356 DAYS OLD

DATE:

(P) By about twelve months of age, you may notice that the small of your baby's back is starting to look more curved than straight. It's easier to see the lumbar curve when your baby starts walking.

(C) What does your baby hope to get out of the actions he intends to carry out? Babies seem to want to try something new, reexperience something familiar, repeat activities they like, and avoid activities with outcomes they don't like. (Hmm. Those seem like our motives, too.)

(S) By baby's first birthday, she may be able to come up with a plan and carry it out in order to solve a problem. For example, if your baby can't find a particular toy, she may dump out all her toys in order to make a thorough search.

Did You Know? Your baby's problem-solving strategy above is called *mean-end behavior*, since baby needs to come up with a strategy (a means) to solve the problem (the end). Mean-end reasoning forms the foundation for all later problem solving.

(P) As parents become better acquainted with their baby, they may find themselves studying her for traces of their genetic contributions. Three general areas may be influenced by genetics: 1. how development is organized; 2. temperament/personality traits; and 3. certain habits.

(C) The intonation that accompanies your baby's expressive jargon (jabber) has the contours of statements (slowly rising and falling), requests (slowly rising and rising again), and commands (sharply rising and falling) found in the English language, or those of her native language.

(S) By age twelve months or so, your baby may be able to use selective attention to filter out noise so she can concentrate on what she's doing. (This is the same hearing that lets them tune you out when you start talking about homework or chores!)

Most of us would do more for our babies than we have ever been willing to do for anyone, even ourselves.
POLLY BERRIEN BERENDS

357
DAYS OLD

DATE:

notes

P The size of your baby's heart at about twelve months is large in relation to the chest cavity, taking up 55 percent of the width of the chest.

C Your baby can begin to understand the properties of a box with a solid lid. As baby watches, remove the lid and put a small object into the box. Open the box to remove the object, then put it back again and replace the lid. Hand the closed box to your baby and tell her to open the box and get the object. By the time your baby is around thirteen months of age, she may be able to get a small toy from inside the box.

S Eager encouragement and enthusiastic praise from parents may not be enough to motivate baby's behavior, especially if the baby tends to be more independent or stubborn. In general, your baby will probably have to be interested in a task before she will put much effort into it.

Check This Out Here are some examples of genetically influenced traits: 1. Development organized around physical, cognitive, or social factors (early or late walker, early or late socializer, et cetera); 2. Some traits include activity level, ability to be soothed, reactions to change, et cetera; 3. Habits like thumb sucking, having an attachment object, and so on.

Week 51 ends

Children feel into their life. Textures of thought, feeling their way into being expressed.
RICHARD LEWIS

358 DAYS OLD

DATE:

359 DAYS OLD

DATE:

By the time your baby is a year old, the antibodies her body has been accumulating since her third month have probably reached 40 percent of adult levels.

There seems to be no harm in letting girls play with traditional boys' toys (like cars and tools), and boys play with traditional girls' toys (like dolls and doll clothes). Dolls help children practice being good moms and dads and tools help children figure out how to fix what's broken.

By about twelve months of age, your baby can communicate that he needs your help. For example, your baby may point to an object on the shelf that is too high to reach, and then look expectantly at the caregiver. (Uh-oh. He's found your chocolate stash.)

In general, babies seem organized to automatically practice movements that provide exercise—like foot-flexing and wrist-rolling—so muscle tone is automatically preserved.

An important problem-solving strategy is persistence. For example, if your baby asks for your help and you do not respond, he may try crying or jumping up and down to see if he can get your attention.

An eleven- to twelve-month-old baby can experience the prevailing pace of life by observing others. If the pace is laid back and slow, your baby may feel relaxed. Likewise, if you are busy and stressed, your baby may become agitated, too.

To be born is like a seed of corn planted for the first time.

DAVID, AGE 9

360
DAYS OLD

DATE:

P One of the most frustrating aspects of child safety is that infants are not automatically bothered by caustic solutions, strong odors, or bad-tasting liquids. And because they can't read, warning labels and the skull-and-crossbones symbol of poison mean nothing to them. Even child-safe caps on medications are not childproof. Put all cleaners, paints, household liquids, and medications under lock and key. If there are any you can discard, do so responsibly.

C The purpose behind some of your baby's intentional behavior is to actively attempt to remove a barrier to a goal. This barrier may be physical (removing a cover or obstacle), cognitive (getting someone to understand what he wants), or social (not listening when others remind him about rules and boundaries).

S Your twelve-month-old baby might solicit help by bringing something to you (like a container she wants opened) or bringing you to something (like a cabinet door that seems stuck).

The trouble with being a parent is that by the time you are experienced, you are unemployed.
ANONYMOUS

361 DAYS OLD	DATE:

362 DAYS OLD	DATE:

P By baby's first birthday, her head circumference may have increased by 33 percent from birth—from about 13½ inches (34 cm) to 18½ inches (47 cm).

C No matter who your child resembles—either in looks or temperament, or both—he will have his own problem-solving style and his own way of doing things. He is himself and always will be.

S Your baby may show some interest in watching TV or DVDs even though her memory is limited and her attention span is only about five minutes. You'll definitely want to select what she watches and when.

P By one year of age, your baby's length at birth has probably increased by 50 percent—from 20 inches (51 cm) to 30 inches (76 cm).

C As your baby's large- and small-muscle skills are developing, he's starting to see how useful they are in solving problems. For example, he can select the best snacks first by moving the yucky ones aside, and if a toy he wants is across the room, he can move to that location.

S Once babies understand that they are distinct from their parents and the objects around them, they seem aware of their own separate existence as people. This insight is a milestone development in the concept of self and identity.

Our children are extensions of ourselves in ways our parents are not,
nor our brothers and sisters, nor our spouses.

FRED ROGERS

363 DAYS OLD   DATE:

364 DAYS OLD   DATE:

P By the time your baby is a year old, her birth weight has probably tripled—from 7½ pounds (3.4 kg) to 22½ pounds (10.2 kg).

C By about this time (eleven to twelve months of age), your baby has become increasingly better at conveying his intentions—what he plans to do or what he wants to do—through vocalizations. (You've gotten better at translating, too, no doubt.)

S Most twelve-month-old babies dislike being restrained. They may even come to resist being strapped into their car seat. This behavior may be motivated by their growing sense of independence.

P By the time babies are a year old, half of them sleep more than four times a day and half sleep less. Babies usually don't sleep less than two times a day and, generally, not more than seven.

C If you play with your twelve-month-old baby, she may begin to learn to associate objects with actual words (like "doggy") or with understood "words" (like "baba" for bottle).

S Your baby's first throws were random—he threw objects because he could. This time his missiles usually come with a message. Your baby may deliberately throw something—at you or around you—to attract your attention. (Watch for the fast-ball, high and inside.)

Adults are obsolete children.

DR. SEUSS

365
DAYS OLD

DATE:

notes

P Your baby's total sleep time per day can range from a low of about seven and a half hours to a high of about eighteen hours per day!

C Never assume your baby will leave something alone just because it is beyond her reach. Also, just because you don't think your baby will be interested in something, doesn't mean she won't want to get at it. The baby of twelve months of age is a curious, resourceful problem solver who can't yet grasp the dangers inherent in stacking, poking, climbing, pushing, or manipulating certain objects. Supervise constantly.

S If you are planning a birthday party for your one-year-old, plan a short, simple gathering at a time when he is most likely to be rested, fed, and happy. Avoid balloons (they're dangerous), busy decorations, entertainment (like a puppet show or a clown), organized party games, too many guests, and too many demands. Remember that babies his age are easily overwhelmed and frustrated. When he becomes tired or tearful, the party's over—and so is Baby's First Year.

Week 52 ends

Your baby's first birthday is here!

Children must have stories.
JOSEPH JOUBERT

Happy Birthday, Baby!

A happy family is but an earlier heaven.

JOHN BOWRING

notes

notes

notes

notes

notes